BREAK UP
EMERGENCY

A guide to transform your BREAK-UP
into a BREAK THROUGH

ERIS HUEMER, M.A.
& CLAYTON WINANS

Grateful acknowledgment is made to Inspired Authors LLC for permission to
reprint a portion of *Thank God I...Stories of Appreciation for EVERY SITUATION*.

ISBN: 978-1-60461-522-7
Library of Congress Cataloging-in-Publication Data is available upon request.

Cover art direction by Curtiss Lopez
Cover design by Curtiss Lopez, Clayton Winans, and Eris Huemer
Typeset in Berkeley, Matrix, and Helvetica
Printed in the United States of America
10 9 8 7 6 5 4 3 2 1

I dedicate this book to all the men
who have entered into my life through one door,
hung out for a while,
and then exited through another.
You all have truly been precious gifts to me.
I wouldn't be who and where I am today if it weren't for you.
—Eris Huemer

I dedicate this book to all the women who I have loved,
liked, sometimes disliked, knew, and thought I knew.
Without you I could not be the man that I have become.
—Clayton Winans

*You don't die of a **broken heart**, you only wish you did."*
—Marilyn Peterson

*"'Tis better to have loved and lost
than never to have loved at all."*
—Alfred, Lord Tennyson

*Things don't go wrong and break your heart so you can
become bitter and give up. They happen to break you down
and build you up so you can be all that you were intended to be."*
—Samuel Johnson

*"Relationships are hard. It's like a full time job,
and we should treat it like one.
If your boyfriend or girlfriend wants to leave you,
they should give you two weeks' notice.
There should be severance pay,
and before they leave you, they should have to find you a temp."*
—Bob Ettinger

TABLE OF CONTENTS

THE IDEA FOR THIS BOOK....

. . . is to help you use your break-up from a romantic love relationship as a soul-transformative experience. To guide you toward not being a victim and the realization that your ex-mate is a mirror reflection of you in more ways than one. To bring you to the point where you see that the relationship was there to bear gifts.

I have blended the very best of the Laws of the Universe and the theories of Carl Jung, Sigmund Freud, Eric Erikson, Depth Psychology, Cognitive Behavioral Therapy, Quantum Physics, Social Theory, Zen, Art, God, Buddhism, Myths, Fairytales, Men, Women, Mystics, Dreams, the world and everyone in it—to name a few—and presented some of their principles here as they apply to 21st century relationships.

By reading this book, and doing the exercises that it introduces, you will get to move further along on your journey towards wholeness, while blossoming into your Best Self.

THE BREAK-UP EXPERIENCE

(They call it a workbook because it works)

In this book are answers to how you can heal your broken heart. If you put the time and effort into yourself—both by reading this book and applying the exercises—you will have a life-transformative experience. I'm secure in this because by committing to the path laid out here, you are demonstrating your intention, a willed and focused thought, to heal your broken heart. And, as with everything in life, if you have an intention, take the steps, and focus on getting there, you will. If you focus on healing your heart, it will be healed. That's just how life works. We shape our own reality, by focusing and then taking the steps to get us to our intentions.

As I see it, you were guided here. You were drawn to this book because your heart has been broken. The real emergency here is that your soul is calling for wholeness. Your true inner self wants to be heard. You have already taken the first step simply by opening this book. No matter what happened to end your relationship, *it was not a complete failure;* it served a purpose. It is your job now to figure out what purpose that was for you, in your life, and to move forward empowered by that knowledge. Your relationship ending does not mean that your life is over; it means that it is about to begin.

I wrote this book because I have been where you are right now. I have had my heart broken and broken and broken. I have been lied to, cheated on, deceived, coerced, cajoled, tricked, cast aside, seduced, corrupted, convinced, and man-ip-u-lated. By believing bad things were *being done to me,* I stayed in my victimhood relationship after relationship, attracting the same kind of men over and over again—all of my Princes turned into Frogs. I was living in La La Land, believing that some day I would find a Prince who would stay a Prince, only to be let down time and time again.

Below is an excerpt of a story that I contributed to an anthology called *Thank God I…Stories of Appreciation for EVERY SITUATION*, which was published in 2008. My piece is all about the men I have chosen and the gifts of those relationships.

Although no one dies in this story that doesn't mean that there isn't a loss of life when you are in a dysfunctional relationship. I felt emotionally and physically imprisoned because I was more concentrated on the relationship than on how I could grow as an individual. Like when inflicted with a disease, I experienced discomfort, pain, and depression. I lost interest in the things I enjoy in life. I found myself wasting days and hours on tears, arguments, sleepless nights and a change in appetite. I felt uncertain about the future. This is my story:

> *The first break up I ever experienced was when my dad left my mom for another woman. He also left my sister and me. How could the man who was my number one, the one I looked up to the most, walk out on me like that? I remember watching him pack his bags and drive away. I was devastated. At that point in my life, I couldn't fully comprehend the effect it would have on me and my future relationships. Here I was, just a teen, beginning to be aware of boys and dating, and I was losing the most important man in my life. I spent the next fifteen years unconsciously trying to replace my dad with a "Prince" who would rescue me and stay happily ever after.*

Mr. Orange...was just cool. He was charming, just like my father. (They all were.) He was a crush. The "relationship" was, in all truth, a figment of my imagination. I swooned over him. He ignored me. I wrote Mr. Orange love letters and built a fantasy world where he was my Prince Charming. Could he be the one? Then, my supposed "best friend" called to tell me that Mr. Orange had just asked her to the school dance. I felt rejected. Is this how my mom felt? Why did my dad choose the other woman over my mother? Why would Mr. Orange choose my friend over me? The only good thing to come of that experience is that I could now relate to how my mom felt when my dad left her. I no longer resented her. Thank God...

Shortly after that, I met Mr. Green. Thank God, Mr. Orange chose someone else! Mr. Green was surely the one! For the next five years, Mr. Green and I fell deeply in and out of love. He showed me how I wanted a man to love me. He was honest, faithful, affectionate, hard working, and would follow through. No, it was not always La La Land. There were times when he drank and changed; he would disappear, but his alter ego whom I named Bob would take his place. Bob and I would fight, constantly. The verbal abuse was traumatizing. I still remembered how much I hated it when my parents drank and fought, and yet here I was in the same relationship. Still, in my need for love, I thought, "Is he the one? Can I live with Bob?" I wasn't sure.

Something in me told me to go, while another part told me to stay. I couldn't decide.

Until...I had an opportunity to move 3,000 miles away to follow my dream. Mr. Green wanted to go with me and get married. The love addicted part of me wanted him to come, of course. I thought I would be crazy to say no. Yet, the realist in me knew that there were things I still needed to do...on my own. I knew I would miss Mr. Green, but I certainly wouldn't miss Bob. He made me feel like I couldn't do things on my own, that I was nothing without him, and nobody would ever love me like he did. I didn't realize at the time that his manipulation would empower me to make the most agonizing decision of my life. I chose to go. Thank God...

Mr. Black... I loved his spontaneity and intellect. He was rebellious without a cause. He gave me books such as **Conversations with God, The Celestine Prophecies, The Alchemist,** *and* **The Artist's Way**—*books that would show me the pathway to my spiritual journey. He encouraged me to buy a journal and begin writing. I became inspired. Was he the one?*

It was the best of times and worst of times. Mr. Black had a shadow side made up of bipolar tendencies, verbal abusiveness, lies, alcohol and drug abuse. He talked down to me, lied, threatened to hit me if I didn't shut up, and didn't commit because he secretly had others (or maybe that was just the baggage of my childhood?). He was a seeker alright, but he often found answers he didn't want to accept.

I talked myself into staying because I learned so much. He soon left me for one of his others. Once again, I felt what my mother must have felt. But this time I realized that my mother was a much happier woman without my dad. She no longer had to live in fear, belittlement, and doubt, and she had found her independence by starting a business of her own. Through Mr. Black's unfulfilled search for knowledge, I found and followed a spiritual path that led me to where I am today. Thank God...

Then there was Mr. Blue. I liked his stability. He was a businessman. Was he the one? He was eighteen years my senior, had an expensive car, took me to nice restaurants, had a sensitive side, was a good friend, and gave me a job. However, he was my boss, so he kept our relationship secret for eighteen months, which ate away at me. He didn't want people to think I had the job because we were together. I didn't care that much about the job, I wanted him to want to be with me. I wanted him to want everyone to know it. I felt like I was living a lie. Each day I woke up wondering, "Will this be the day when we no longer have to hide the truth?" He just couldn't admit, and wouldn't commit, to the reality of our relationship.

Then one day I couldn't take it anymore. I quit my job and "we" were suddenly over. I no longer was living in a secret, and most of what I learned about business and success I learned from him. Thank God...

Through that job I met Mr. Yellow. He was incredibly artistic, talented, and free. One look at him and my knees buckled. Was he the one? We had so much fun together. We went on long nature hikes, he taught me about organic food, and brought me to my first yoga class. He wrote me songs about love and soul mates and promised that we would be together forever. I was envisioning marriage, 3.2 kids, and a white picket fence. He taught me how to find my inner voice and not only speak it but put it on paper.

But this La La Land was not meant to last. He broke-up with me—over the phone—without warning. He said he needed space, a chance to find himself. I was devastated. I was convinced that he was my soul mate, my life partner. I didn't understand why he left, so I began writing about it in my journal, and out came a first draft of a self-help book with remedies on how to heal your broken heart. Thank God...

Then there was Mr. Gray. I wasn't convinced that he was the one, but he said he was. I chose to play along and believe him—it began to work. My biological clock began to go tick-tock, tick-tock. He was a recovering addict and had embraced spirituality. I enjoyed that we could talk for hours and hours about common ideologies and beliefs. He was rebuilding his life and I thought he included me in that process. It felt like we were starting over together. "This is it," I said. "Yes, I want to get married." I told him he was the one. He said he wasn't. He needed a ninety-day break to think it over. He never got back to me with an answer. He was the one, all right. The one that could only focus on himself. Thank God...

I was exhausted. What was going on? Was there really a "one"? How many more break-ups was I going to have to endure?

That I chose these men, or let them choose me, was not their fault. At the time, I was unable to see the relationships for what they were and my part in them. When enough was enough for me, I decided to allow the Sleeping Beauty within me to wake up and recognize that I had been repeating the same patterns over and over again. The only reason I felt so hurt and depressed, I now could see, was that I was living in a romanticized fantasy of what the relationship coulda, shoulda, woulda been. I was driven and bound by my emotions, which distorted the reality, and kept me off balance. I realized that by living in victimhood I had been disempowering myself. I felt my gut telling me that there was a way out of feeling the way I did and it was time for me to get it together.

I finally realized that the only way things would ever change is if I took charge of my life and **helped me help me.** Others may act as guides but it was me, myself, and I who had to do the work. Ultimately, I realized, the only things I could control were my own choices and actions. I was determined to figure out how to find balance and got help from different sources such as books, seminars, therapy, 12-step programs, spirituality, friends, family, and meditation, etc., etc., etc.

One day someone suggested that I write a gratitude list of at least ten things that I am grateful for and to include my ex. She suggested I do this every day. I took her suggestion and began writing in my journal. I began seeing the gifts of attracting Mr. Gray into my life, and the rest of the men of my past as well. Without them, and the unfortunate circumstances of my relationships and their ending, I would not be where I was, growing and changing and learning to stand on my own two feet.

Writing down the things that I am grateful for allowed me to focus on the positive things in my life. It helped me move out of the past negative into the future positive. From this I became consciously aware of the benefits and gifts that I received. Writing my gratitude list took the edge off of the heaviness that I was feeling. I did this every-day until I began living in gratitude. I continued this process in all aspects of my life, even today. Through this I learned that the **BREAK** in my relationships were experiences that would bring me **UP** in my evolution process. It was up to me to determine how fast I was going to grow and evolve. Writing a gratitude list is just one of the exercises that I have experienced myself that will be shared with you in this book.

Healing my broken heart did not happen overnight, but becoming more conscious did. I discovered many healing tools through my break-ups, and as I worked them they evolved into the exercisies you will find in this book. The more I worked them, the more I understood myself. They inspired me because I began to see results. I felt better, more personally powerful. I became confident and secure. I began to realize that I was not a victim. I found the gifts that my relationships brought me.

My friendships became more solid and deeper than ever before. My work relationships grew stronger, and I became closer to my parents and sister. I began to create a future that had more meaning to me. This inner work put me on my path to discover my individual self and who I want to be in this world. And I began to like, finally, the woman I was becoming. From my so-called "failed" relationships, I found my life's purpose and the power that lies within.

I have a master's degree in counseling psychology, am a relationship counselor and life coach, and have done thousands of hours of research into the human condition—mainly how it relates to the interaction between couples. I have compiled information from multiple sources via graduate studies, books, lectures, interviews, life coaching and counseling sessions with clients, etc. Guiding others to have break *through* experiences after a break-*up* has become my passion, my education, and my job. I would like to share with you these exercises that you can use to create a better life for yourself. I hope you will allow these tools to help you on your journey toward finding fulfillment and wholeness. My greatest desire is for you to take control of your life and find your strengths, your voice. No matter what has come before, you can create the life you want to live and become your Best Self. As difficult as this time may be, you are in your situation *because you put yourself there.* Every person we attract into our lives is a mirror reflection of who we are. We choose to attract them into our lives to awaken hidden, denied, and unconscious truths about ourselves. They come into our lives for a reason.

If you choose to accept this and find within yourself the gratitude for what your ex (and every other ex-friend or lover) awakened in you, you will be on a path to becoming more balanced, focused, and conscious. If you acknowledge that whatever the other person "did to you" can be overcome, then you will be able to heal and move on. It is all about coming to understand the lessons your experience brought you.

Basically, we all have two choices: we can live in fear or we can live in love. You can choose to be a victim or you can choose to take charge of your life. You can choose to cry day in and day out and have people feel sorry for you because your ex did this and that to you, or you can choose to see the lessons this person gave to you, learn from them and move on. If you choose the victim path, you will keep repeating your same patterns, behaviors, and attract the same kind of partners into your life. If you choose to take responsibility, you allow the **Break** to take you **UP** to your next level of personal development.

You have asked for some answers on how to heal, and here they are.
I now invite you to embark on your journey...

THE BREAKS

Today my heart is broken. My dreams of living a life of getting married to MR. GRAY, having children & living a spiritual journey together have been shattered.

I have pain today & I feel loss. I don't even feel like it has really hit me yet. It hurts most in the morning & when I go to bed at night.

O

-noun
1. *Informal.* The way things happen; fate.
2. A trying or troublesome circumstance.
3. Scheduled interruption. Turns of events.

The Seven Stages of transformation—
from Breaking Point to Break Through.

Breaking Point—*when you or your partner realizes that your relationship is no longer serving you and at some time in the future it must end.*
Break Up—*when the relationship is ended.*
Break Out—*the physical separation and the actions surrounding the break-up.*
Break—*a time out while you collect your thoughts and feelings.*
Break In—*when you embark on an internal quest to learn from your relationship and grow.*
Break Even—*when you gain knowledge through which you come to accept your past.*
Break Through—*the point at which you find gratitude and reach for your Best Self.*

YOU ARE HERE

"Words and hearts should be handled with care
for words when spoken and hearts when broken
are the hardest things to repair."
—Anonymous

If you are still grappling with the end of a relationship, you probably recognize yourself in one of these seven stages of transformation. Which stage you are in, for the purpose of this book, does not matter. You might still be trying to break-up with your ex, yet you feel so attached because you like his company. You might have broken up six months ago and still feel down and out. Maybe you have let go of the relationship on many levels but subconsciously you have not. You might be in a slump, not being able to move on and meet someone new. Maybe you met someone new and are repeating the same patterns. No matter where you are, I suggest that you begin at stage one and work your way through stage seven. You never know what you will discover about yourself as you move through the exercises and apply what each stage has to offer.

These seven stages are here as a guide to help you transform your break-UP into a break THROUGH experience.

Catherine O

When I was a little girl everything I saw around me screamed love, love, love—all you need is love. I grew up believing this. Its what I lived in my waking days and dreamed about while asleep at night. But, one relationship after another failed for one reason or another. It wasn't the pain that hurt so bad. That in time lessened. My heart became callused, less sensitive. It was the not knowing HOW to deal with the pain, HOW to get through it. It was WHEN was it ever going to end. It was WHERE would I be if and when this pain did end. Would I ever have a new relationship? If so, would it just be the same (mistakes, problems, arguments, person with a different name) just to end again?

FROM BREAK-UP TO BREAK THROUGH

TRANS*itional in***FORM***ation motiv***ATIVE EXPERIENCE**

> *"To be or not to be, that is the question"*
> —William Shakespeare

You are no longer Mr. or Ms. So and So's significant other. All too often, when a relationship ends, we dwell on what our ex did, is doing, or how to win him back, but the process this book will take you through will reveal to you why you attracted your ex into your life in the first place, and help you take responsibility so that you do not repeat the same behaviors and relationships. The good news is, often times we have to go through an identity crisis in order to change.

To stop these repetitive behaviors, you have to accept that all your relationships have something to teach you. That's what they're about. If you are going to allow your break-up to be a transformative experience, you have to turn inward and look at your own patterns, your own behavior, who you attract into your life and why. You have to know your stories and own your part in them. You have to be willing to discover different parts of yourself and begin to realize the dreams you have left unfulfilled. This is not about blaming yourself, it's about finding your own inner power and keeping the focus on the only thing you can change: you.

During this time of self-evaluation and change, you might experience fear, confusion and intense emotions. If you do, I suggest that you write down or put a voice to whatever you're feeling, figure out what you can do about it, and do it, and then turn it over to whatever

Higher Power you believe in. Feelings are just feelings. By acknowledging them and dealing with them they will dissipate and become less frightening.

Throughout this book, I will even prompt you to write down your thoughts and feelings for self-evaluation. This will allow you time to let go of fears and emotions that are overcoming you. If you focus on your intention to heal your broken heart—you will.

"To thine own self be true."
—William Shakespeare

HOW TO USE THIS BOOK

This book is not the be-all and end-all answer to all of your problems. No book can deliver that. But it does share specific, time-tested exercises that can help you get over your loss.

Use what works for you. Try the suggested exercises, questionnaires, and essays. Answer them with whatever comes to you, without worrying about being judged. This is your book—you don't have to share it with others unless you want to. When you find an exercise that helps, continue to use it as long as it is helpful. The exercises might seem difficult, time consuming, scary, or even silly at times. You might even say to yourself, "I don't want to do this one—I'll skip it." Don't. Just do it. You paid for this book—get your money's worth. These exercises not only can't hurt you, they have a cumulative effect of bringing you clarity and self-knowledge, and from that kind of understanding you will change and grow.

"God helps those who help themselves!"
—Hezekiah 6:1

These exercises are here to help you help yourself. There is no set time frame you have to work in; however, don't rush through or stall this process. Find your pace so that you can achieve the self-awareness that is offered in these exercises.

"Take the first step in faith.
You don't have to see the whole staircase, just take the first step."
—Dr. Martin Luther King Jr.

Are you ready to take your first step? Let's begin.

REFLECTION

Mirror, mirror on the wall, who's the _____ of them all?

"Know thyself."
—Socrates

re_flec_tion_ [ri-**flek**-shuhn]
—noun
1. the act of reflecting or the state of being reflected.
2. an image; representation; counterpart.
3. a fixing of the thoughts on something; careful considera-tion.
4. a thought occurring in consideration or meditation.

The first step in the process of any significant personal change is reflection. Reflection is about being self-aware. It's about being honest with yourself and getting to know the different parts of you—the good and the bad, the ugly and the beautiful, the kind and the mean, and your past and present experiences.

Remember.
Explore.
Find.
Learn.
Examine.
Contemplate.
Think.

**To your own self be true,
because you're the only one that truly knows you.**

Self-reflection is about becoming more aware of your conscious and unconscious, which make you who you are. Being aware of your personality, your behavior, the way you react to situations and people—all of this will allow you to better understand your story—your experience—your truth—your life.

We all have glimpses, flashbacks, and remembrances of our past—our first years, our school years, our teenage years, our first kiss, significant relationships, our travels, our surroundings, and all experiences that brought us to where we are today. The more we reflect, the more self-knowledge we gain. It all makes up what becomes our inner décor.

We all think we know ourselves pretty well, but I'm talking about becoming more deeply aware of the real you. The masks you have worn to survive in your world, or to make others happy, your strengths and your weaknesses, your light side and your dark side, your fears, your dreams, your resentments, your insecurities, your values, etc. This is about getting to know everything about yourself.

Who we are is always a complex web of who we have met, how we feel, our tastes, our wants, our needs, our desires, our do's, our don'ts. All of it. We cannot control everything that happens to us in the world. We can only direct ourselves as to who we want to be, and do the best that we can do. Life is a matter of moment by moment decisions. To help you practice making better decisions and better choices, we will use the tool of self-reflection throughout this book. By looking back you can see more clearly as you move forward.

WRITING AS A WAY OF HEALING

"We write what we don't know we know."
—Anonymous

One of the greatest forms of self-reflection and healing is writing. The act of writing is an invitation for you to dive deep into your psyche and reflect. You never know how your unconscious might answer. It gives you the opportunity to have an inner dialogue with what is going on inside of you. If you do not censor what you write, and just let it flow through you, your own words can take you deeper and deeper into yourself. Writing during hard times can be a way of working through your problems. It can help you deal with challenging emotions and feelings and help you figure out what steps to take next. It is a form of meditation and can de-stress you. It may help you understand your break-up by leading you to answers of your own questions. It is helpful to write about things that you do not want to share or discuss with others.

By writing, you can keep from bottling up your feelings inside of you, which can create emotional problems in the future. When you write about your break-up, and the story that you are experiencing, your life can transform. Throughout this book you will be asked to write the thoughts and feelings of your reflections in the form of essays, inventories, questionnaires, and journal entries.

"Writing eases my suffering...
writing is my way of reaffirming my own existence."
—Gao Xingjian

Intro to Inventories

in_ven_to_ry_ [in-*vuhn*-tawr-ee, -tohr-ee]
-noun
1. a tally of one's personality traits, aptitudes, skills, etc., for use in counseling and guidance.
2. a formal list of the property of a person or estate.

Throughout this book you will also be given the opportunity to do inventories. Inventories help us get to know ourselves better. They allow us to be aware of our personality traits, feelings, fears, and aptitudes, so that we can get a better understanding of what is going on in us. As we become involved in doing them, our unconscious reveals to us things about ourselves that we have been unaware of. Inventories allow us to get to know certain things we will have to face within ourselves in order to move on. They help intense feelings dissolve, and can help us come to terms with the fact that **feelings are not facts** and that they do change. Inventories are a great tool for freeing yourself from the pain of the present.

Your Book

"My aim is to put down on paper what I see and
what I feel in the best and simplest way."
—Ernest Hemingway

Get yourself a journal or small notebook, which I call YOUR BOOK. YOUR BOOK is where you can write down everything that is going through your head about your ex, ex relationship, you, and your life: questions, answers, promises, apologies, thoughts, feelings, gratitude, to do lists, etc. Keep YOUR BOOK with you as much as possible during this period. It is important to do this because during the early stages of a break-up, the thoughts in your head can seem confusing and overwhelming. Writing them down will allow you to let them out and then have them later on for reflection if needed. Feel free to write anything and everything that you want to. There are at least five important reasons to keep YOUR BOOK:

1. By writing about whatever's going on, you are not taking it out on your ex, which saves you the humiliation of confrontation and/or rejection.
2. By writing, you get your feelings out of your head, which gives you clarity.
3. It gives you a cooling off period.
4. It keeps the focus off of the drama and into healing.
5. It helps you move on.

Examples of things that you can write in YOUR BOOK are memories, gratitudes, goals, and etceteras.

Memories
The way it was, it was.
(past)

As a first exercise with YOUR BOOK, write down a memory, any memory, from your past relationship.

Memories can be both negative and positive, but no matter how difficult your past situation was, it is a part of what made you who you are today. You can use your memories to better understand yourself and your current behaviors and patterns.

Gratitudes
It's great to be grateful
(present)

Write down the things that you are grateful for in your life at present.

Gratitude is when you can see the negative and positive in the situation. No matter how difficult your situation feels right now, there are things in you life that you can be grateful for. Gratitude can be your catalyst to change. Any time you are overwhelmed by your emotions, write your gratitudes. I suggest that you write a gratitude list of ten things a day that you are grateful for. These things can be large or small.

Goals
To Do's and How To's
(future)

Write down the things in your life that you feel would be beneficial for you to deal with to better your life. Write down the steps that you need to take in how to achieve this. Goal setting can give you the focus you need to achieve them.

Etceteras
Etc., Etc., Etc...
(anytime)

Write whatever you want anywhere, anyway, anytime.

IN CLOSING

Remember, no *one* formula works for every single person. Speakers, therapists, coaches, healers, and sponsors might try to impose their perspective onto you as the answer. The only answer that I have for you is to listen to your own intuition and be honest in what works and is right for you. You are your number one healer and physician. *Help you help yourself.* I am here as your guide to show you different paths that you can take. It is up to you which one you choose.

THE BREAKING POINT

1. I feel like **I AM** responsible for other peoples choices. I can control them into believing that I know whats best for them.
2. I feel obligated to **HELP** people + solve their problems/issues. I feel **ANGRY** when they can't seem to help me.
3. I find myself attracted to needy people

4. I check on people.
5. I usually put the focus on my boyfriend's need + passions instead of my own.
6. Afraid to let other people be themselves + let events happen naturally.

1

-noun

1. The point at which a person, object, structure, etc., collapses under stress.
2. The point at which a situation or condition becomes critical.

The Breaking Point stage is when you or your partner realizes that your relationship is no longer serving you and that at some time in the future it must end.

He loves me—He loves me not.
She loves me—She loves me not.
Or: What do you do when
you run out of flower petals?

If you've ever had a break-up then you've had a breaking point. It may have happened overnight, but most likely it has been a long time coming. Maybe you were aware beforehand, maybe you weren't. If you weren't, you were probably in denial. Either way, you can't have a break-up without a point of breaking. What your breaking point was, whether you did the breaking, or your partner did, doesn't really matter. It happened. Your job now is to be honest with yourself about everything surrounding this breaking point and your responsibility in it. This is where the healing begins.

ENTERING THE GATES OF LA LA LAND

"La La Land—that's where books and movies are supposed to take us."
—Anonymous

la-la land (lä'lä)
1. A place renowned for its frivolous activity.
2. A state of mind characterized by unrealistic expectations
or lack of seriousness.

Beginning a new love relationship is like entering the gates of a Secret Garden. It's a place where a caterpillar creates its cocoon for the butterfly to escape its chrysalis and flutter around in your stomach. Falling in love feels like ecstasy. The bee's wings, in frenetic motion, cause a buzzing sound in your ear. Life instantly begins to have meaning. Two birds in flight soar into the clouds. Your heart beats faster. Entangled and entwined. You are floating on air, and your possibilities seem endless. You experience a sense of vitality that you never felt before. The love you feel sparks a flame deep within your unconscious. Supplies of oxytocin, endorphins, dopamine, serotonin and other neurotransmitters are at high levels. Then you come crashing back to earth. You know your ABC's and the birds and the bees. Its love in La La Land.

We long for love in La La Land. This began when we were little children and discovered stories, myths, songs, books, poems, movies, television, and their fairy tales within. It permeates our world.

"We have been poisoned by fairytales"
—Anais Nin

Jane E.

Three months, three weeks, two days, twelve hours ago I met my fiancé (but whose counting?). It was AMAZING! I hadn't taken a vacation in over two years. I won the sales competition at work and won a free cruise to Mexico. And there he was—tall, dark, and relatively handsome. And he, from across the room, picked me! It was love at first site—for seven days and six nights. We took snorkeling excursions, drank margaritas at cruise ship pool side, dressed up for romantic dinners at sunset, he serenaded me backed by a mariache band. We had the same interests, similar backgrounds, and education. By the fifth night his warm brown eyes looked deep into mine and he said, "I love you, Jane. You are the one for me. I want to spend the rest of my life with you." My knees buckled at his every word. He was my Prince Charming.

Your La La Land Essay
You had me at hello

Write your story from a La La Land perspective, remembering only the good times—how you first met, your first date, how he wooed you, the qualities you most loved about them, how you envisioned your life together would be, etc.

Once upon a time... (Insert your story here.)

_____

_____

_____

_____

_____

_____

_____

_____

_____

_____

_____

_____

_____

_____

_____

_____

_____

_____

_____

_____

_____

_____

_____

_____

_____

_____

_____

Continue free writing on these subjects in YOUR BOOK.

La La Land is not a place exactly. It's that falling in love time when both people in a relationship are on their best behavior, while they are still getting to know one another. We hold onto the memories of this time—when we first met. Love in La La Land is not all bad. In fact, it can be one of the most wonderful times in life. However, if you believe that all happiness and pleasure can come from this love, then you are living in the myth of La La Land. If you believe that there is a Mr. or Ms. Perfect out there, then you are living in a happily ever after that does not exist.

La La Land is a good place to visit, but not to live in. It is a false ideal of love. It's the land of unrealistic hope. It's non-reality. Perhaps the other person has not yet shown you his true self: his anger issues, that she is in debt, that he has substance abuse problems, that she has issues from her childhood, that she is a workaholic, that he is an over-achiever or underachiever, that she doesn't want to be monogamous, that he is not financially reliable, that he is emotionally unavailable, psychologically unstable, or a dreamer with one foot in reality.

We can float along in La La Land for a while, but at some point, inevitably, we will start seeing characteristics, behaviors, and parts of the person we didn't see before. We will also begin to see parts of our true self that we had forgotten about. It's not that they, or we, intentionally hid these things, maybe just tried to leave them behind. But as surely as day turns to night, they will surface. And reality will set in. If you deny that your love has two sides, a positive and a negative, you just prolong the inevitable fall. You also have two sides. That's how life works.

CROSSING THE THRESHOLD
INTO REALITY LAND

"Love is not blind; it simply enables one to see things others fail to see."
—Anonymous

Where did we get this idea of happily ever after? Everywhere! Romantic love is deified. Hollywood movies, poetry, songs and novels continue to make us believe and wish that this perfect fantasy-like love could become a reality. We continue to look for our lover to provide us with all meaning in life. We go to sleep at night dreaming and praying for this kind of love to happen. This false idea of love ignores the groundwork that relationships require. Many people go through their love relationships half asleep and unconscious. Many times the relationships end up falling apart.

*"Some think that **love** is all flowers and **good** times, but I think that **love** is more than just that. **Love** is the **bad**, as well as the better, not lived alone, but a journey together."*
—Anonymous

By coming back into Reality Land you begin to see that each person has two sides, a dark and a light. In varying degrees we all are nice and mean, kind and cruel, generous and stingy, funny and sad. The reason why people are attracted to one another is because of their similarities and differences. It's the yin and yang. One is outgoing, one is shy. One is brave, one is timid. One is a leader, one is a follower. Both are adventurous. Both are homebodies. Both are artistic. Both are spiritual. One person can't balance their checkbook while the other is meticulous with their finances. Each owns a part of the other that the other disowns in himself because it is uncomfortable for him to deal with.

When a relationship goes past the La La Land phase and into Reality Land, you have to question whether you can be with this person's particular dark side. The answer is not necessarily no. Whether you realize it or not, your lover is a mirror to you and is introducing you to unknown aspects of yourself and bringing them to consciousness. What you don't like about him—these are all aspects of you, and this person is giving you a chance to face them. Sometimes it's just too difficult to work through the challenges the other person brings into your life and you have to call things off, but you can always learn from the unconscious aspects of yourself that are being presented (PRESENTed). When you are able to accept these presents, that's love—that's what makes life worth living in Reality Land.

Jane E. (continued)

Well, turns out that he wasn't my Prince, and not so charming. Our cruise on the "Love Boat" ended. Things were great for a while, but slowly, things changed. We lived in different cities. The long distance relationship was almost as exciting as the cruise. I quit my job, sold my house, and moved 1,500 miles away to be with him. I moved into his fully decorated house and he didn't want me to put any of my decorations out. I then quickly realized that what I thought was a few harmless margaritas on a cruise ship vacation was actually a nightly, sometimes all-daily, habit. After a few cocktails he turned mean. It wasn't that he was a bad guy, he just wasn't the guy I thought I knew. Even though we had similar interests, we didn't have enough in common to sustain a relationship. The fantasy had ended and the reality had begun. I no longer had my friends and family right there. I felt needy, clingy and lonely. I made myself believe that this would pass—but it didn't. We did.

I Like You I Like You Not Questionnaire

What drew you to your ex?

_____

_____

_____

_____

What similarities did you have? (personality, family background, education, etc.)

_____

_____

_____

_____

_____

What differences?

_____

_____

_____

_____

_____

Have you experienced these similarities and/or differences in your past relationships? [ ] yes [ ] no

If yes, name those similarities and differences.

_____

_____

_____

_____

_____

_____

What aspects about yourself does your ex mirror back to you?

_____

_____

_____

_____

_____

What parts of yourself do you disown that your ex owned in himself?

_____

_____

_____

_____

_____

What actions can you take to start owning those aspects in yourself? And when are you willing to begin to take those actions?

_____

_____

_____

_____

_____

_____

Continue free writing on these subjects in YOUR BOOK.

Unfortunately, many people cannot accept these presents. They do not use their relationship for inner growth. Instead, once La La Land is done, they become complacent, aware of flaws in the other, realize that the love is not all fun and games, and Reality Land has begun. They don't want to deal with the facts. They decide that staying together through difficult human reality takes too much work. This leads to conflict in the relationship, often causing a heart-breaking ending. They give up and break-up.

Of course, sometimes a break-up is necessary for the ultimate well being of both parties, but often it's well worth the effort to stay and work through the difficulties, the realities that arise.

THE REVOLVING DOOR BETWEEN LA LA LAND AND REALITY LAND

"To love is to suffer. To avoid suffering, one must not love.
But then, one suffers from not loving.
Therefore, to love is to suffer; not to love is to suffer;
to suffer is to suffer.
To be happy is to love.
To be happy, then, is to suffer, but suffering makes one unhappy.
Therefore, to be happy, one must love or love to suffer or suffer from
too much happiness."
—Woody Allen

Those of us who repeatedly seek out La La Land but never stay for Reality Land are stuck projecting our values, dreams, wants, and needs onto other people hoping they are *who we want them to be*, but *not who they are*. We break up before ever breaking through. Once we break up it can be too painful to look at the reality of what the relationship was. Sometimes we ignore or have difficulty acknowledging who the person we were with actually was. We don't see who we were in the relationship. But it is so important not to ignore the truth and to see reality for what it was, not just what you perceived it to be.

The first reality is that there is no such thing as a "perfect" relationship (except in romance novels or fairytales). The perfect guy or girl is a delusion. The truth is that your relationship was perfect in the sense that you chose to be there and there are lessons to be learned. You might not have been able to learn these lessons without the relationship.

Once you step out of false hope and unrealistic fantasies into Reality Land, it can feel like a tough place to be in at first. But, the truth is that, only when you look at yourself and your relationship from the Reality Land perspective do you give yourself the opportunity for growth.

If you continue to idealize a lover after a break-up, you will be faced with many problems. You may feel like you will never meet another person like them again. This will make it difficult for you to move on.

The Idealized Ex Questionnaire

What makes you feel like your ex is more special than other people?

_____

_____

_____

_____

Do you feel like you will never meet a person like your ex again?
[ ] yes [ ] no

If you feel like you will never find love with another person like you felt with your ex, explain why.

_____

_____

_____

_____

Who in your life (past or present) has the same qualities as your ex?
Describe the person and their qualities.

_____

_____

_____

_____

Describe the feelings and experiences you had with your ex that you
don't think you could have with another person.

_____

_____

_____

_____

What was your relationship really like, not your idealistic fantasy
(both the positives and negatives). Write your TRUE story, not your
fairytale.

_____

_____

_____

_____

_____

_____

_____

_____

_____

_____

Continue free writing on these subjects in YOUR BOOK.

If you continue to idealize a lover after a break-up, you may feel like you will never meet another person like them again. This will make it difficult for you to move on. In order to get past idealizing, you must get your head out of the clouds and feet back on the ground. Ask friends and family to remind you what the relationship was really like—both the negatives and the positives. When you have these conversations write down 2 or 3 things, both positive and negative, about your past relationship and your reflection on these things. You can write this in YOUR BOOK for later reflection. And don't worry about imposing. These conversations are not about you getting **attention**; they are about you having an **intention** of not repeating your same patterns and behaviors.

PROJECTIONS

I see you, you see me
I love me, you love you

"I have a feeling that being in love sometimes means
the projection of your desires onto another person."
—Eric Braeden

We are attracted to each other in love relationships because of our projections—both positive and negative. We are drawn to certain characteristics in others that we haven't accepted in ourselves. Or we lack certain characteristics in ourselves and are attracted to those characteristics in others. When someone else's behavior angers us, it is because this same thing lives within us but we have not taken responsibility for it. When we admire a quality in someone else, it is usually a quality we lack in ourselves and wish we had. When we fail to find what we are looking for in ourselves, we search for it in others. We unconsciously try to complete ourselves through another person.

> *"Everything that irritates us about others can lead us to an understanding of ourselves."*
> —Carl Gustav Jung

This can be a puzzling concept for a lot of people. We have a difficult time recognizing our own strengths and weaknesses, which causes us to project them onto others. We are afraid of becoming all that we are capable of becoming (i.e. our Best Self). We are also afraid of facing our demons (i.e. negative qualities we don't allow ourselves to see). It is easier to see these qualities in others than to find and face them in ourselves.

The dramas that we have in relationships in the external world are the dramas that we have in our internal world. They are entwined and interconnected. The flaws that you see in him, if you look hard enough, are flaws that are in you as well. You might not express exactly the same behavior or action, but it is still something within you getting awakened. For example, the fact that your ex is an alcoholic, or his drinking bothered you, does not mean that you are a drunk. However, if you were to look deeper at this, you would ask yourself "Why would I allow myself to attract this type of a person into my life? What is it from my past? (i.e. were my grandparents or parents alcoholics?) There can be many different answers to this question.

The Projectionist Questionnaire

If your lover left you, ask yourself and your heart what parts of yourself you have been ignoring or leaving. Doing this can replace focusing on why your ex left you. If your ex was afraid of commitment, ask yourself what parts of you are afraid of commitment. Or in what ways are you not committing to yourself?

What projections do you have on your ex?

_____

_____

_____

_____

_____

_____

_____

_____

_____

_____

_____

_____

_____

_____

_____

_____

How can you take back the projections that you have placed onto your ex and relate them to yourself?

_____

_____

_____

_____

_____

_____

_____

_____

_____

_____

_____

_____

_____

_____

_____

Repeat this exercise with any of your other exes. Look for any similarities and differences in your projections. How can you own those projections in yourself?

Continue free writing on these subjects in YOUR BOOK.

The point is, he is gone now, but you are still here.

As the saying goes, when you have one finger pointing at someone else, you have three pointing back at yourself. If you want to change something in another, you should look to see if there is something in you that needs to be changed. When someone pushes your buttons or you put them on a pedestal for owning qualities that you admire, recognize where you have these qualities in yourself. You can begin to provide for yourself what you are expecting the other to provide for you.

THE CODE OF CODEPENDENCY
OUR SECRET SOCIETY OF II

"Always be a first-rate version of yourself,
instead of a second-rate version of somebody else."
—Judy Garland

Many couples become so enmeshed with one another that they become one. Each partner believes that their lover is necessary for life. Their relationship becomes everything to them. They forget their own individuality, becoming so preoccupied with making their relationship work, and they forget about their own hobbies, family, friends, and everything else important to them. This is where the curse of codependency begins.

Whenever a person becomes fused with another and loses her identity, she becomes codependent. You can also call this relationship addiction. Relationship addiction happens when a person believes that a lover is necessary for life. She does not have her own identity but derives it from someone else. But nobody, no matter how outstanding, can continue to fulfill all your needs. When the relationship falls apart the addicted person becomes even more lost. For her, being "in love" is really a matter of being addicted to another person.

People in codependent relationships do not realize that they are in an unhealthy relationship. They are so focused on their partners, on fixing them, attending to them, and deriving their own sense of worth from them, that they begin to lose their sense of self and what their own needs are.

A person who experiences a break-up in a codependent relationship often feels inadequate and worthless and feels like the decision was one-sided (not theirs). Sometimes there is a violent ending. They might feel animosity for the other person and they might try to inflict pain. The codependent usually tries to manipulate the person into coming back. They might seek solutions outside of themselves and self-medicate with drugs, alcohol, or a new lover. There might have been a lot of denial from the start, a fantasy of what the love was really like. They might not have a realistic view of the other's commitment.

If you believe that you have codependent tendencies, such as various degrees and layers of caretaking, low self-worth, repression, obsession, controlling, denial, dependency, poor communication, weak boundaries, lack of trust, anger, sex problems, and violence, I suggest that you begin to acknowledge them. Don't be ashamed or hard on yourself in recognizing these traits, because most of us have them. The important thing is to see them and then stop acting on them.

"Tweedle-Dee said to Tweedle-Dum,
'Now that we're together, we can have some fun.'"
—Anonymous

How Codependent Are You? Questionnaire

Make a list of your codependent traits:

_____

_____

_____

_____

What can you do to not act out on these codependent traits?

_____

_____

_____

_____

What are some of the things that you only did with your ex and you would like to continue doing but might not feel comfortable doing alone?

_____

_____

_____

_____

If you don't want to do them alone, who could you do them with?

_____

_____

_____

_____

Continue free writing on these subjects in YOUR BOOK.

Forget Mr. Perfect. He Doesn't Exist.

In order for you to be in a relationship fully, without getting lost, you must stop expecting that anyone will be your one stop, be all, Mr. or Ms. Perfect. No one can be there 24-7, even if they want to. No one can cure all of your childhood wounds, save you, fix you, and you cannot fix him. In every healthy relationship you need to:

- Take time for yourself.
- Not allow yourself to fuse with the other.

> To love and have romantic love is not to become fully addicted to the relationship and to become fused with the other. It is to keep your separateness and autonomy.

What was
Our, ourselves, ours
Is now
Me, myself, and mine

One of the many problems of being addicted to love is that we can become so enmeshed that we forget our own goals, dreams, and wishes. We forget that we have our own life's purpose to fulfill. We get so wrapped up in the relationship that even though we know it is not the right one for us we remain in it. Sometimes only our friends and family are able to see the reality of it. But no matter how much they tell us, we only come to terms with the reality after we step away, breathe, take a look back, and reflect.

"If I try to be like them, who will be like me?"
—Yiddish proverb

LIVING IN REALITY LAND
MARRIAGE, 3.2 KIDS, AND A WHITE PICKET FENCE

"Every time I close the door on reality it comes in through the windows."
—Jennifer Unlimited

Living in Reality Land can be difficult. It's the day to day, paying the bills, deaths in the family, kids get sick, mortgage needs to get paid, one person is ready to change jobs, one is starting on a spiritual path the other is not, one might not want kids, one might not feel as sexually connected to the other, one might lose their job ... Reality land is all areas of your life: Financial, Family/Friends, Career, Recreation, Personal Growth/Spiritual, Love/Relationship, and your Environment. One area may be going well, another may be just okay, while even another seems unbearable. In Reality Land, you have to find your balance, whatever that is for you, to create a good, healthy environment.

Natalie S.

Before I was pregnant with my first child, my relationship with my husband was strained at best. But then, while I was pregnant, things seemed to get better. Then with the birth of our little girl, there were a few months of the most amazing time in our relationship, since we had first met. I never wanted it to end, but it did. No sleep at night, baby crying, my maternity leave ended and I had to put her into day care, financially we were struggling, and our love life was non-existent. He spent less and less time at home with me and the baby and more and more time at work. His excuse was the bills needed to get paid. But, I knew that he just didn't want to deal. It was no longer fun and games. It was stress and work. I tried to get him to therapy and he refused. We made it through a few more years and another baby before we got a divorce.

Reality Land Essay
Honey, I'm home

Write your story from a Reality Land perspective. What was your relationship really like.

Once upon a time... (Insert your story here.)

_____

_____

_____

_____

_____

_____

_____

_____

_____

_____

_____

_____

_____

_____

_____

_____

_____

_____

_____

_____

_____

_____

_____

_____

_____

_____

_____

_____

_____

_____

_____

_____

_____

_____

_____

_____

_____

Continue free writing on these subjects in YOUR BOOK.

Reality Land Questionnaire

When thinking in Reality Land terms, how satisfying was your relationship?

_____

_____

_____

_____

_____

What were all of your areas (Financial, Family/Friends, Career, Recreation, Personal Growth/Spiritual, Love/Relationship, your Environment) in your Reality Land like then?

_____

_____

_____

_____

_____

What are all of your areas (Financial, Family/Friends, Career, Recreation, Personal Growth/Spiritual, Love/Relationship, your Environment) in your Reality Land like right now?

_____

_____

_____

_____

_____

What would you like all of your areas (Financial, Family/Friends, Career, Recreation, Personal Growth/Spiritual, Love/Relationship, your Environment) in your Reality Land to be?

_____

_____

_____

_____

Continue free writing on these subjects in YOUR BOOK.

"The best things in life are free until your credit card bill is due."
—Anonymous

DENIAL STAGE—this isn't happening to me!
de·ni·al　　[di-**nahy-uhl**]-*noun*
1. disbelief in the existence or reality of a thing.
2. refusal to recognize or acknowledge; a disowning or disavowal

IGNORING RED FLAGS
HOW I ALMOST DROWNED IN THE UNDERCURRENT OF LOVE

"Sign, sign, everywhere a sign
Do this, don't do that, can't you read the sign?"
—Five Man Electrical Band

People do not betray us, we betray ourselves. Throughout a relationship, there are signs. Signs of what the other person is feeling. Signs of what the other person is doing. Signs of the truth that is unspoken. These signs are warnings like red flags at the beach when the under-tow is too dangerous. These signs, if not confronted, can exist for days, weeks, months, even years, stagnating the relationship.

If you ignore the red flags you could get pushed out to sea or even drown. These signs can come in many forms:

- He no longer calls ten times a day
- You used to have romantic dinners together, now it's strictly take-out pizza
- All his time is no longer yours
- Your sex life is down the tubes
- You suspect she is having an affair
- He is verbally or physically abusive
- You argue constantly
- He drinks or uses drugs to excess, etc.

Red Flag Questionnaire

Were there any red flags in your last relationship that you chose to ignore?

[ ] yes [ ] no

If yes, list them:

_____

_____

_____

_____

_____

_____

_____

When did you first notice the red flags?

_____

_____

_____

_____

What did you do about them at that time, if anything?

_____

_____

_____

_____

_____

What is it about you that allowed this behavior to continue?

_____

_____

_____

_____

_____

Where does this behavior exist in other areas of your life? (Work, friends, family, etc.)

_____

_____

_____

_____

_____

When this situation comes up in your life, how can you handle it differently?

_____

_____

_____

_____

Continue free writing on these subjects in YOUR BOOK.

Red flags are not a bad thing. I'm not suggesting that you should have left when the first one arose, just that these can be cautionary signs that guide you through the rough roads of a relationship. It's up to you to read them and how you act upon them.

Melissa S.

One day as I was sitting alone in the kitchen, my boyfriend walked in, opened the fridge, took out a carton of milk, and started drinking out of it. It struck me as funny for a moment because this is something that I had not seen him do in a long time. When we first got together, he didn't own any drinking glasses, so I bought him some and proceeded to correct this behavior. But there it was again. After all my work! I confronted him, which seemed to make him drink more straight out of the carton. As he finished the last few drops, set the carton back into the fridge, and told me our relationship was over. I have to say that I was in shock. But, being the intelligent woman that I am—I shouldn't have been. The signs were there, all around me, for months now. At first small things, then medium, then larger—as if he was begging me to break up with him. But, finally, I guess he just had enough.

WHEN ENOUGH IS NOT ENOUGH

The Breaking Point is the moment, or moments, of your relationship when one member has had enough but just can't seem to end it.

Breaking Point Questionnaire

What was the breaking point in your relationship?

_____

_____

_____

_____

How long did this breaking point period last before the actual break-up?

_____

_____

_____

_____

What were the circumstances surrounding this breaking point?

_____

_____

_____

_____

In reflection, what are your feelings about this period in your relationship?

_____

_____

_____

_____

How would you handle a situation like this differently in the future?

_____

_____

_____

_____

Write about the moment you realized that there was a breaking point in your relationship. (What happened, what was said, what the moment looked like, what it felt like for you, etc.)

_____

_____

_____

_____

Continue free writing on these subjects in YOUR BOOK.

IN CLOSING

We all have breaking points. When they happen, they happen. But, when THE breaking point happens, it can seem painful and shocking—even if it has been coming for a long time. When enough is enough, it's enough. Be thankful for this because sometimes we are better off alone than living in La La Land or creating our own hell in Reality Land (a.k.a—codependent behaviors and unhealthy projections). Sometimes, the best we can do is break-up and move on.

THE BREAK-UP

- I am feeling sad.
- I am feeling lonley
- I am feeling scared
- I am feeling for all of the lessons that I am learning.
- I am feeling A N G R Y !!!!! SHOCK!
- I am feeling like I am in denial.
- I am feeling mad at myself.
- I am feeling totally sad.
- I am feeling confused.

II FACTS

- Mr. Gray broke up with me. - or 90 day Break.
- Mr. Gray said that I should date other people.
- My father left my mother for another woman.
- My mom proposed to my dad - Not the other way around.
- Mr. Gray and I gave each other our keys back.
- Mr. Gray and I aren't in a relationship anymore.
- My rent is due on the first.
- I have a sister and love Her.

III. MY EXPECTATIONS

- I expected Mr. Gray to be loyal
- I expected Mr. Gray to follow through w/ wanting to marry me -right away
- I expected Mr. Gray! to be honest & communicate
- I expected Mr. Gray to want to have
- I expected Mr. Gray to call + pers
- I expected Mr. Gray to want to t
- I expected Mr. Gray to want to

IV How my best self could do things

- Not be so controlling
- Live in the relationship one day a
- Not be focused on marriage
- Keep my big mouth shut when
- Not rush into commitment premature
- follow my intuition

2

Break-up \Break"-up`\

-noun

1. Disruption; a separation and dispersion of the parts or members.

The Break Up stage is when the relationship is ended by one or both parties.

Adiós. Ciao. Au revoir. So Long. Farewell. Auf Wiedersehen. Good-bye.

Now that you've gotten past the breaking point, its time to break up. The break-up stage can be fearful, even to some degree to the person doing the breaking up. Whether its amicable or one sided, it is still difficult to both people involved (the fear of no more companionship, cohabitation, communication, or sexual relations). Rarely are break-ups without any difficulty or remorse. If so, be thankful. If not look at your situation and try to find the positive in the negative because if you don't, nobody will.

Michelle P.

Moments after I heard those words, "It's not you—it's me," I wanted to throw up. How did we get to this moment? We were so in love. I thought he was the one—my happily ever after. My head was spinning with thoughts and emotions. I could not collect them enough to say a word. As I drowned in silence, I realized that he was still talking. As the blah, blah, blahs became words again, I realized that he was taking the blame for everything. I remember thinking, "God, he must really want out of our relationship." He never, once, took the blame for anything in our relationship. When I finally came to my senses enough to speak, I heard myself say, "can't we try to work it out?" His response was, "I think it's best that we don't."

HAPPILY EVER AFTER—**NOT!**

"It is only possible to live happily ever after on a day-to-day basis"
—Margaret Bonnano

From a La La Land perspective there are no break ups—it's happily ever after. Well, this is not La La Land. Break-ups are a simple fact of life. We live in an age where nearly half of all relationships end in break-ups and half of all marriages end in divorce. 59% of Americans say that they have been through a break-up at least once in the past ten years. 2.2 million people under the age of thirty-five get divorced every year in America. So, you are not alone.

These days, being in a monogamous healthy relationship is not guaranteed. Nor is it required. More and more people are opting out for other alternatives. It is not a rite of passage—it is a right of choice. If you choose it, it is your responsibility to make it work. If anyone tells you that being in a relationship does not take work, then they are probably not in a relationship.

IT'S A BREAK UP NOT A BREAK DOWN
JUST BECAUSE THE OPERA IS OVER
DOESN'T MEAN THE FAT LADY HAS SUNG

Most people believe that breaking up means losing the other person. This might be true physically, but the experiences and knowledge you gained through your ex are there for you forever. They are a part of who you are today and who you are about to become. Your past relationship is something that you attracted into your life to help you evolve. It is something that has happened because it is part of your life's journey. You have made your choices that you can't take back. So, use them to grow and move forward. If you don't like the consequences of your actions, then don't repeat them.

"Take a second out to think about this:
in your life you search and search for the right person for you.
Every time you break up with someone you get
one step closer to that person.
You should look at moving on as getting closer to meeting the one."
—Ian Philpot

Your break-up is official. It's real. However, the experiences you had in your relationship were also real. It's part of who you are and your life's story.

What was the reality of your relationship? Who was the person you were with? What kind of person were you in the relationship? What were the real dynamics of the relationship? That's what we'll be looking at in this chapter.

First, I'd like you to answer the following questions from a Reality Land perspective.

"Being entirely honest with oneself is a good exercise."
—Sigmund Freud

It's Over 'Cause It's Over Questionnaire

Your relationship just ended after how long? _____

Who broke up with whom? _____

What was the reason for your break-up?

_____

_____

_____

_____

From your perspective, what events led up to the break-up?

_____

_____

_____

_____

How did your break-up happen? (Ex. Words said, time of day, place, situation, etc.)

_____

_____

_____

_____

How long were you and your ex growing apart before it ended?

_____

_____

_____

_____

How did you react during and after the break-up?

_____

_____

_____

How are you reacting right now?

_____

_____

_____

_____

List four words that describe your ex.

_____

_____

_____

_____

What was the most dramatic moment in your relationship?

_____

_____

_____

_____

What was the happiest or greatest moment in your relationship?

_____

_____

_____

_____

What are the things that you did that your ex complained about, asked you to change, and you did not change?

_____

_____

_____

_____

What did your ex do that you complained about and asked him to change, and then he didn't?

_____

_____

_____

_____

How did you communicate in your relationship: (Check all that pertain to you)

[ ] Nag	[ ] Attack	[ ] Shut down
[ ] I am always right	[ ] Calm	[ ] Good Listener
[ ] I am great at it	[ ] Passive	[ ] Aggressive
[ ] Unforgiving	[ ] Forgiving	[ ] Patient

How did you handle conflict and arguments in your relationship?

_____

_____

_____

_____

How did your ex handle conflict and arguments in your relationship?

_____

_____

_____

_____

Who initiated most of the conflict and arguments? How? Why?

_____

_____

_____

_____

Who was most likely the one to mend these conflicts and arguments?

_____

_____

_____

_____

How do you feel about your ex today?

_____

_____

_____

_____

Continue free writing on these subjects in YOUR BOOK.

Whatever your experience, you are in the place where you are right now because you chose to be, whether consciously or unconsciously.

"*I don't miss him,*
I miss who I thought he was."
- Anonymous

Your Break-up Essay
What ever happened to happily ever after?
Or:
You had me at good-bye.

Get it all out! Feel free to vent. I suggest that you do.

Once upon a time... (Insert your story here.)

_____

_____

_____

Continue free writing on these subjects in YOUR BOOK.

SHOCK STAGE—*What's is happening to me?*
shock [shok]
-noun
1. a sudden and violent blow or impact; collision.
2. a sudden or violent disturbance of the mind, emotions, or sensibilities

LOVESICK BLUES

There's a sickness that's going around.
It's not the common cold. It's not the flu.
It's love.

You feel ill, depressed, sick to your stomach, anxious, and exhausted. Your body aches, you can't concentrate, you can't eat, you can't function, and you can't sleep. Your love obsession is your sickness and you believe that getting a dose of that love again is your only cure. Nothing else matters: family, friends, career, health, finance, recreation, and internal growth. You just want that love back. Sound familiar? Maybe you've got "it." Maybe you've got the lovesick blues.

Question is, how do you get rid of it? If only you could take a pill (having them say "I love you"). Even a placebo sounds good right now (even a hello would do). Then you could get on with life.

How Lovesick Are You? Questionnaire
Following is a checklist of symptoms to see how serious your love sickness is (Check the box that applies):

- *Can't concentrate [ ] severe [ ] mild [ ] non-existent*
- *Can't complete tasks [ ] severe [ ] mild [ ] non-existent*

- Can't sleep [ ] severe [ ] mild [ ] non-existent

- Can't stay awake [ ] severe [ ] mild [ ] non-existent

- Can't eat [ ] severe [ ] mild [ ] non-existent

- Can't stop eating [ ] severe [ ] mild [ ] non-existent

- Can't stop crying [ ] severe [ ] mild [ ] non-existent

- Can't stop talking about my ex [ ] severe [ ] mild [ ] non-existent

- Can't work [ ] severe [ ] mild [ ] non-existent

- Can't go anywhere or do anything [ ] severe [ ] mild [ ] non-existent

- Not taking care of my body [ ] severe [ ] mild [ ] non-existent

- Not taking care of my kids/pets [ ] severe [ ] mild [ ] non-existent

- Not taking care of my bills/house [ ] severe [ ] mild [ ] non-existent

- I call my ex obsessively [ ] severe [ ] mild [ ] non-existent

- I check my voice mail obsessively [ ] severe [ ] mild [ ] non-existent

- I do drive-byes [ ] severe [ ] mild [ ] non-existent

- I think about getting even [ ] severe [ ] mild [ ] non-existent

- I think about killing myself [ ] severe [ ] mild [ ] non-existent

- I'm afraid of being alone [ ] severe [ ] mild [ ] non-existent

- I'm afraid of losing my mind [ ] severe [ ] mild [ ] non-existent

- I'm drinking more than usual [ ] severe [ ] mild [ ] non-existent

- I'm doing drugs more than usual [ ] severe [ ] mild [ ] non-existent

- I'm smoking more than usual [ ] severe [ ] mild [ ] non-existent

If you have any other symptoms (not listed above) that feel debilitating to you, list them below:_____

_____

Continue free writing on these subjects in YOUR BOOK.

If you checked severe on a number of these questions, or even one, if you're having any thoughts of suicide, please seek professional help.

> *"Get busy living, or get busy dying."*
> —Stephen King

There is no one cure for the lovesick blues. But you do have two choices: Live in this pain (like an ocean washing over and drowning you). Or, live with this pain (like a river, you go with the flow). First you have to admit that your relationship is over so that you can begin to heal.

Make a list of constructive things you can do to lessen your lovesick blues symptoms.

FEEL
RIDING THE ROCKIN' ROLLERCOASTER OF LOVE

> *"Life is not all lovely thorns and singing vultures, you know."*
> —Morticia Addams

Immediately after the break-up, it is totally natural to be filled with mixed emotions. The goal is to get past this. However, for now, realize that you are human. During this period, recognize your rollercoaster of emotions—Up, down, good and bad. You may feel angry, sad, lonely, tired, scared, upset, afraid, confused, ashamed, numb, or even relieved.

> *"You have a right to your thoughts and feelings.*
> *Your feelings are always valid."*
> —Iyanla Vanzant

During the first few days your emotions will probably be more intense. A tool that seems to work for many is to physicalize whatever emotion they are feeling. Punch and kick the air, sleep all day, hit your sofa with a pillow, shop, go to the gym. Yell at an empty chair and pretend that your ex is there and tell her how you feel. Tell him the things you wished you had said. These are temporary, quick-fix solutions.

Do whatever you need to do for yourself. Just do it. All you have is right now, this moment.

Emotions Questionnaire

The next two pages are filled with words for many different emotions. Which ones do you find yourself feeling the most? Circle the ones that stick out for you.

Confident	Angry	Hopeful	Agonized
Victimized	Spirited	Free	Pained
Sunny	Perplexed	Loving	Impulsive
Glad	Sore	Pessimistic	Thrilled
Satisfied	Lousy	Loving	Paralyzed
Sad	Shaky	Secure	Upset
Frisky	At ease	Dull	Shy
Guilty	Elated	Liberated	Anxious
Impulsive	Kind	Sure	Cowardly
Certain	Accepting	Indecisive	Dynamic
Alone	Lost	Helpless	Happy
Alive	Good	Serene	Hurt
Wary	Passionate	Nosy	Excited
Fearful	Aching	Lonely	Loving
Pained	Fatigued	Grief	Tragic
Certain	Relaxed	Empty	Overjoyed
Snippy	Unique	Anguish	Lifeless
Brave	Panic	Curious	Cowardly
Playful	Tearful	Unhappy	Serene

The Break Up

Daring	Offended	Guilty	Bright
Frightened	Desperate	Wronged	Glad
Tormented	Quiet	Mournful	Threatened
Doubtful	Spirited	Bored	Determined
Fortunate	Terrified	Grieved	Powerless
Hostile	Bitter	Heartbroken	Eager
Energetic	Curious	Ashamed	Rejected
Calm	Content	Terrible	Tender
Surprised	Doubtful	Festive	Sulky
Miserable	Stupefied	Blessed	Empty
Receptive	Afflicted	Upset	Disappointed
Brave	Scared	Alienated	Cheerful
Lucky	Bad	Hateful	Enraged
Appalled	Diminished	Dull	Quiet
Uneasy	Thankful	Reserved	Lousy
Crushed	Bright	Neutral	Great
Incapable	Skeptical	Cowardly	Joyous
Uncertain	Devoted	Unsure	Wonderful
Deprived	Spirited	Confused	Positive
Alarmed	Afraid	Indifferent	Anxious
Sorrowful	Boiling	Confident	Alive

After you are finished circling all of the emotions that pertain to you, write each one down and what it means to you. (Feel free to add any I might have missed.)

_____

_____

_____

_____

_____

_____

Do you feel this way often? _____

Have you ever felt this way before? _____

When do you feel this way? _____

Where do these feelings show up in your life? _____

How does it feel to feel this way? _____

Choose the most significant emotions you want to change and take some action to shift them.

Continue free writing on these subjects in YOUR BOOK.

In time you will be able to move on, but only through an honest inventory of your feelings. There is nothing wrong with feelings just as long as you deal with them constructively.

> *"Feelings, nothing more than feelings,*
> *Trying to forget my feelings of love."*
> —Morris Albert

Feelings Inventory

If you are still feeling a roller coaster of emotions, do a feelings inventory. This tool can always be here for you. The importance of the feelings inventory is knowing that your feelings are not facts.

Once you have completed the feelings inventory you might want to read it out loud to someone you trust, either in person or over the phone. This can be very helpful. If you talk about your growth, you will grow. But that is up to you.

The feelings inventory takes the following steps:

1. State how you are feeling. (I am feeling sad, angry, scared.)
2. State whatever facts are on your mind (the who, what, when where, WHY). (My boyfriend cheated on me, he left me with a sack of bills, and he gave me an STD.)

3. State what your expectations were in the relationship. (That we would get engaged, that he would be faithful to me forever, that he would repay the money he borrowed from me.)

4. State how your Best Self would have you do things differently. (Not rely on him, keep doing the hobbies I did before we met, not lend him money, have protected sex.)

Your Feelings Inventory

Now it is your turn to do your Feelings Inventory. Continue writing in each section until you do not have anything to write anymore. Do not censor yourself.

1. Feelings

I am Feeling _____

I am Feeling _____

I am Feeling _____

I am Feeling _____

I am Feeling _____

I am Feeling _____

2. Facts

- _____
- _____
- _____
- _____

3. The Expectations I had

- _____
- _____
- _____
- _____

4. What my Best Self would have me do differently

- _____
- _____
- _____
- _____

Continue free writing on these subjects in YOUR BOOK.

Remember, all feelings pass, both good and bad. Anytime your feelings overwhelm you, use this exercise and find the lessons in them.

Feeling Collage

Another exercise that can help bring to the surface the way you are feeling is collaging. Collaging is a therapeutic process that allows your unconscious to speak through different images. To collage, cut up different pictures from magazines that express how you are feeling (sad, angry, even furious), and paste them together on a poster board.

> "Usually when people are sad, they don't do anything.
> They just cry over their condition.
> But when they get angry, they bring about a change."
> —Malcolm X

ANGER STAGE—*Why is this happening to me?*
an·ger [ang-ger]
-noun
1. a strong feeling of displeasure and belligerence aroused by a wrong; wrath; ire.
-verb
4. to arouse anger or wrath in.

Tanya A.

Dear Ex,

You said you loved me, in sickness and in health, for richer or poorer, for better or worse, till death do us part. I wish you were dead you ******* son of a *****. I hope you and your lawyer rot in hell! I hope that young, stupid ***** you left me for gets Toxic Shock Syndrome from the boob implants that I know our retirement fund paid for. I hope your children never know what an evil ******* their lying, conniving, two-timing absentee father you was and is. But since it's so obvious to everyone else, they probably will.

P.S. I hope your **** rots off from the venereal diseases your 22-year-old lover will certainly give you—if she hasn't already!

With best wishes,
Your EX

"I try to talk to you but I don't know what to say. I am afraid you don't want me to say anything. So I don't. But inside of me there are words waiting to come out. And tell you how I feel—like how I miss you. And how I love you despite my broken heart. And how I need you in my life. And especially how much I want you. But those words may forever stay in my heart—locked inside. Sometimes I sonder if there are words locked inside you, too…but I'll never know."
—Anonymous

Angry Letters

"A friend of mine once said that hate
is too important an emotion to waste on someone you don't like."
—Joe Williams

Write two angry letters.

1. Write an angry letter to yourself. Vent all of your feelings to yourself in this letter. Tell yourself how angry you are at your

ex, why you chose him in your life, and how angry you are about the situation. Allow yourself to express yourself.

2. Write an angry letter to your ex. DO NOT SEND IT UNLESS YOU ARE ABSOLUTELY CLEAR ON YOUR REASONS. However, if you do, recognize what your expectations are: Do you have an agenda (ex. Hurt him because he hurt you).

3. Now send the letters to yourself, either via regular mail or e-mail. Whatever you do, don't open the letters for at least 48 hours to give yourself some time to reflect.

You've Got Mail

When you open the letters, look at them for where you can take responsibility in the relationship. Realistically, honestly, and truly look at them. Own your own Sh*t, and begin to see how you can grow from it.

Now that you are done with the letters, rip them up, delete them, or burn them—whatever you would like to do with them! Again, I'd caution you against sending them to your ex.

"When we live with resentment toward another, our hearts close down. Letting go of our resentment frees us from placing blame on them and allows us to look toward ourself for peace."
—Tigress Luv

BALANCING THE MOTION OF EMOTION

"Just as your car runs more smoothly and requires less energy to go faster and farther when the wheels are in perfect alignment, you perform better when your thoughts, feelings, emotions, goals, and values are in balance."
—Brian Tracy

Emotions are energy in motion. Up and down and up and down. When you are driven by emotions, you distort what is really happening. You become out of balance. When you are driven by the emotion of love, you are able to see only the positives. When you are driven by the emotion of fear or hurt, you are able to see only the negatives. Just be aware that whenever and whatever you are feeling—angry, sad, depressed, etc.—there is a complementary opposite emotion happening—peaceful, happy, elated, etc.

You might be driven by intense emotions right now; but it is your choice on the reactions that you have. If you were infatuated with your ex and he broke up with you, you will feel remorse, bereavement, grief, loss, and sorrow over the loss of pleasure. When you are over someone and you leave them, you feel elation, excitement, ecstasy, joy, and gain.

Life has its ups and downs—happy sad, optimistic pessimistic—it's a never-ending balancing act. If you see that your feelings are out of balance between the negative and positive, the following exercises can help you understand why you are feeling this way. Then you can choose to stop. Information is power. It is up to you.

Feelings, Nothing but Feelings Inventory

For each of the out-of-balance emotions you are feeling, find a way to counter balance it in your day-to-day life. In this Feelings, Nothing but Feelings Inventory, name the feeling, why you are feeling this way, what you can do to balance out this feeling, and when you can do it. Example:

- *What am I feeling? (I am feeling lonely, depressed, angry.)*
- *Why? (Because my ex is no longer here to hug me. I miss physical contact.)*
- *What can I do? (I can hug my kids, a friend, or my mom.)*
- *When can I do it? (When they get out of school or when my mom gets out of work.)*

Part of the purpose of this questionnaire is to give you an opportunity to get in touch with what you are feeling. Just sit back and think about your feelings and how you can balance them.

Feeling	Why?	What can I do?	When can I do it?

Continue free writing on these subjects in YOUR BOOK.

"I can control my thoughts.
My feelings come from my thoughts.
I can control my feelings."
—Wayne Dyer

Balance Inventory

1. Write down all of the things that you believe you have lost since your break-up. For example you might feel like you lost companionship, intimacy, sexual passion, financial support, a confidant, a mentor, their smile. Keep writing in "The things I lost" column until you can't stop. The more you write, the more this will help.

2. Once you are finished writing in that column, write down the things that you have gained since the break-up in "The things I gained" column. For example you might find that you have gained time with friends, family, peacefulness (no fighting), strength to financially support yourself, self awareness, confidence to stand on your own two feet, your smile. Keep writing until you can't stop.

3. You may soon discover that all of the things you believe you have lost can be replaced by you, someone else, or something else in your life (just in a different form). In the "How it can be replaced in my life" column, write how you can replace these things in your life. If you are missing affection you might have a cuddly dog. If you are looking for companionship and a confidant, who are your friends? If you need a mentor, might it be your boss or a co-worker? If you are looking for financial support, take control yourself, speak to a banker, or get an accountant or broker.

The things I lost	The things I gained	How it can be replaced in my life.

Continue free writing on these subjects in YOUR BOOK.

I LOVE THEM—I LOVE THEM NOT

We all have things that we love about the people in our lives. We all have things that we hate about the people in our lives. Each person is a mirror reflection of who we are. What we see in them is also visible in ourselves (even if it is in a different form). Many times we choose not to see it. You might love that your partner is cuddly, attractive, creative, smart, loyal, a good lover, witty, outgoing, and adventurous. You might hate that your partner is not affectionate, allows her addiction to rule her life, isn't committed to bettering himself, has no money, is scattered, lies, is messy, has different spiritual beliefs than you, or judges you. It is important that you can find these qualities within yourself (the ones you hate and love) because you have them.

Has anyone ever told you that you have this trait and/or quality? It might not be in the same form as your ex, but it is there. Think about it and you will find it.

For example: He has an addictive behavior. Where in your life do you have an addictive behavior? You might believe that she is not committed to herself. Where in your life are you non-committed? If he lied to you, where were you lying to yourself or where do you lie? If she judged you, how do you judge yourself or others? If you think that he is funny, who has told you that you are funny? If you love his intelligence, can you own your intelligence?

I Love Them—I Love Them Not Inventory

Fill out the inventory on the following page. Do as many qualities in each section as you can. Feel free to continue this exercise in YOUR BOOK.

Things I HATE about my EX	Who has seen this same trait in me even if they have not said it?	In what way do I own this same trait in myself? (You do!)	How can I not use this same trait in my life?

Things I LOVE about my EX	Who has seen this same trait in me even if they have have not said it?	In what way do I own this same trait in myself? (You do!)	How can I use this same trait in my life?

Reality Check Questionnaire

Who was the first person you fell in love with? How old were you?
How long did the relationship last? Explain the details.

_____

_____

_____

_____

_____

_____

_____

_____

How old were you in your first sexual encounter? _____

Who was your first sexual encounter with? _____

Explain how that experience was for you. _____

_____

_____

_____

_____

How many people have you had sex with? _____

Do you wish you had sex with more or fewer people?
[ ] more [ ] fewer

Why?

_____

_____

_____

_____

What are your feelings around sex today? What do you think about sex?

_____

_____

_____

_____

Write a list of your past significant love relationships.

_____

_____

_____

_____

Have you been married before? [ ] yes [ ] no

If yes, how many times? _____

What are your views on marriage?

_____

_____

_____

_____

What was your parents' marriage/relationship like?

_____

_____

_____

_____

What was your ex's parents' marriage/relationship like?

_____

_____

_____

_____

What do you consider love to be and look like? What does love mean to you?

_____

_____

_____

_____

Have you ever cheated on someone? [ ] yes [ ] no
If yes, how did you feel about it?

_____

_____

_____

Has anyone ever cheated on you? [ ] yes [ ] no
If yes, how did you react?

_____

_____

_____

_____

How many times has someone broken up with you? _____

How many times have you broken up with someone? _____

Have you been divorced before? [ ] yes [ ] no

If yes, how many times? _____

Were there children involved? [ ] yes [ ] no

If yes, who got custody and how did this affect you?

_____

_____

_____

_____

What was your most difficult break-up and the reason?

_____

_____

_____

_____

What was your easiest break-up and the reason?

_____

_____

_____

_____

How is your last relationship similar to your past relationships?

_____

_____

_____

_____

Do you continue to attract the same types of men/women into your life?

[ ] yes [ ] no

Explain:

_____

_____

_____

_____

What patterns are you repeating?

_____

_____

_____

_____

Continue free writing on these subjects in YOUR BOOK.

*"Whatever relationships you have attracted in your life at
this moment,
are precisely the ones you need in your life at this moment.
There is a hidden meaning behind all events,
And this hidden meaning is serving your own evolution."*
—Deepak Chopra

IN CLOSING

Happily Ever After more times than not only occurs in fairy tales. That's not saying that you can't be happy in a relationship. It just means that you have to have a realistic idea of what happiness is. Now that your relationship is over, it is a perfect time for you to reevaluate your own happiness. What made you unhappy in the past that you can change by not repeating again in the future? Right now you might be surrounded with feelings that are at times overwhelming. This chapter has begun to help you deal with your feelings, but it's up to you to continue to get your emotions in balance for a more healthy you.

THE BREAK OUT

I'M

FREE!!!

TO do What I WANT.....

3

-Phrasal Verb
1. To emerge or escape.
2. To ready for action or use.
She is going to break out of her prison.

The Break Out is the physical separation and the actions surrounding the break up.

Breaking Up 101:
What they tell you in all the other break up books,
but it never ever hurts to read it again.

The break out stage can be a time of conflicting emotions. You might even feel, at times, like you are in a tug of war with yourself. One moment you might be upset over your break-up. At other moments you might find yourself elated with your newfound freedom because you don't have to deal with the difficulties that permeated your relationship. During this time it is important to be aware of falling back into your same old patterns and self-destructive behavior.

BE AWARE OF THE BIG BAD WOLF

"We hope for the day when Ms. Love will overcome her drug issues and present no risk of harm to herself or others.
—Gloria Allred

Now that you are out here in the real world, single and seemingly "alone," you might want to escape your problems by fleeing back into La La Land. It is obvious that you might naturally be inclined to dive into some self-destructive behavior. Drinking alcohol more often than usual, overeating, undereating, overspending, gambling, chain smoking, sleeping around, overworking, etc. A great example of self-destructive behavior is drinking seven Cosmopolitans, not being able to walk because your head is spinning, ending up with your head in the toilet, and passing out on your cold bathroom floor. (Very Cosmopolitan.)

Self-Destructive Behaviors Questionnaire

Do you have a tendency to act out on any self-destructive behaviors? [ ] yes [ ] no

If yes, what are your self-destructive behaviors?

_____

_____

_____

_____

Are they working for you? [ ] yes [ ] no

If not, what can you do to stop them?

_____

_____

_____

_____

If you persist to act out on self-destructive behaviors, please seek help. There is emergency contact information in the Emergency Contact Information of this book to help you.

We take many roads to try and escape our disappointments and betrayals. Self-destructive behavior might help you hide your feelings momentarily, but it does not make the feelings or problems go away. It just allows you to hide your head in the sand, and sabotage any situation into being worse than it already is. Trying to erase the pain through self-destructive behavior will only make matters worse. Prolonged self-abusive behavior is nothing more than a detriment to your physical and mental well being and will get you nowhere. You are your own worst enemy. Eventually, you are going to have to deal with your feelings.

In order to get through the pain, you have to feel it. There is no better time for this than now, but it's your choice. One important thing to remember is: **FEELINGS ARE NOT FACTS. ALL FEELINGS, BOTH GOOD AND BAD, PASS.** Do all things in moderation, so you can wake up in the morning, feel good about yourself, and know that you did the best that you could do.

REBOUND

"I was looking for love in all the wrong places
Looking for love in too many faces."
—Waylon Jennings

It feels good to get romantic attention after you experience a break-up. Rebound flings can be fantastic, thrilling, and exceptional. You feel butterflies once more. Everything is new and exciting. The nature of this relationship is refreshing after all you have just been through in your prior relationship. No more in-depth conversations about nothing that spiral into arguments. No more lonely nights spent together. No more ignoring major things while overfocusing on the minor ones.

You are in La La Land and you are enjoying the ride. When you were in love, then lost, and are instantly in love again...when you fall head over heels in love with someone quickly after a break-up...that is a rebound. Rebounds can be fun, but they rarely last.

Rebounds sometimes happen when you are addicted to a fantasy of what a relationship should be like. I strongly suggest taking some time to be balanced before getting back into the mix of dating. You don't want to find yourself making the same mistakes or attracting the same person.

If you were to break your leg running, would you go out and run the next day? Or, would you give your leg some time to heal and question yourself as to what happened on your run and why it broke? By sitting with the pain in your leg, resting, and allowing it to heal, you can learn what you did wrong and try not to repeat the same thing the next time. Why not do this with yourself after your break-up?

However, as with everything in life, there can be exceptions to the rule. There is no one correct time frame for moving on from one relationship to the next. How quickly you move on is up to you and you alone. Be your own barometer. If you decide to be in a rebound relationship, enjoy yourself but be careful.

Bounce Back Questionnaire

If you do choose to be in a relationship shortly after your last, ask yourself the following questions:

Am I a serial monogamist? Do I have a history of going from relationship to relationship?
[ ] yes [ ] no

Am I trying to fill a void right now?
[ ] yes [ ] no

Is my ex in a rebound relationship and am I trying to prove a point?
[ ] yes [ ] no

When I am out with this person, do I think about my ex often?
[ ] yes [ ] no

Are my old patterns coming up again?
[ ] yes [ ] no

If the answer to any of these questions is **YES,** then you might want to reconsider what you're doing. I am not saying that you should not go out and have fun. But, this might be a good time to take a time out from dating to reflect and grow. If your old patterns are coming to the surface again, and you are not ready to change them, then it is, simply put, too soon to be in love again.

Even if you much prefer being in a relationship over being single, it's really important to learn how to be secure alone and have fun on your own. If you need someone to go to the movies, dinner, and the gym with, ask a friend. That's what friends are for. And, what about getting comfortable with your independence? A healthy relationship can only be built by two strong individuals, and becoming strong in yourself takes time.

Batteries not included
Or:
With a little help from my friend

"What do I do when my love is away?
I'm going to try with a little help from my friends."
—Lennon & McCartney

Masturbation. Masturbation. Masturbation. Now that you're alone, take the time to pleasure yourself because if you don't, who else will? Masturbation is a useful tool to relieve stress and tension while allowing oneself pleasure. There are many forms and practices, which we will not detail in this book. But, please feel free to do your own research and find what works for you.

> BARGAINING STAGE—I promise I'll be a better person *if*...
> **bar·gain·ing**
> - v. *intr.*
> 1. To negotiate the terms of an agreement, as to sell or exchange.
> 2. To engage in collective bargaining.
> 3. To arrive at an agreement.

Diana T.

After we broke up, even though it was mutual, I began to miss him. Everywhere I looked were reminders of our relationship—people places, things. All keys to unlocking my heart's pain and frustration. Then one day I had a thought—"Why not just be friends?" This would be the best of both worlds. We could hang out and do friend things—go to dinner and the movies, talk on the phone sharing our day-to-day lives without all the relationship stuff that caused all the drama that ended us in the first place. And it worked for a while (a couple of weeks)...

JUST FRIENDS OR JUST ENDS?

You might still want to be friends. However, many use the "just friends" concept as a manipulative tool to win the other back, to continue the same committed relationship benefits such as sleeping together, because they aren't 100% sure that they want this relationship to end but they still want to date other people, or because they feel lonely and want to continue to do the same things together.

Calling, e-mailing, texting, and IMing are prime examples of communication tools that can be abused and can cause more harm than good. Every time the phone rings your heart skips a beat because you think it's him. But, it's not.

The phone is not your friend right now. I suggest not contacting your ex if you just want attention, are in need of affection, or because you are lonely. And most certainly do not drink and dial. Even though it is not against the law, it will get you busted. Only contact him if you have a specific issue to discuss—something that is of importance to you both. Otherwise you risk only more heartache. Think of this as if you are in jail—you only get one phone call, don't waste it.

Just Friends Questionnaire

Have you ever tried the "just friends" concept? [ ] yes [ ] no

What were the positives?

_____

_____

_____

_____

_____

What were the negatives?

_____

_____

_____

_____

_____

Are you doing the "just friends" concept now? [ ] yes [ ] no

What are the positives?

_____

_____

_____

_____

What are the negatives?

_____

_____

_____

_____

Have you ever called or tried to contact an ex after the two of you broke up? [ ] yes [ ] no

Did they answer? [ ] yes [ ] no

If no, how did that make you feel?

_____

_____

_____

_____

If yes, did you get the response that you were looking for?
[ ] yes [ ] no

How did that make you feel?

_____

_____

_____

_____

Are you thinking of contacting your ex now? [ ] yes [ ] no

If yes, list the ways that it will serve you.

_____

_____

_____

_____

If you take the venture to call, notice what your expectations are. (How are you expecting him to respond? What do you want him to say to you? Why do you feel the need to call?) Write it all down.

_____

_____

_____

_____

If you imagine calling him, what would it be like in a La La Land perspective?

_____

_____

_____

_____

If you imagine calling him, what would it be like in a Reality Land perspective?

_____

_____

_____

_____

If calling him isn't a positive, make a list of all of your supportive friends and family members who you can contact instead:

_____

_____

_____

_____

Another note of caution: Be careful not to take advantage and overcall friends and family to seek "therapy" and complain about your ex. This can keep you in victimhood and away from self-realization/actualization and put stress on your relationships.

What are some things you can do instead of contacting him? (Examples: go shopping, to a movie or even a double feature, exercise, write, learn more about yourself, plan a trip alone or with friends, watch television, go to a friend's house, prepare a nice meal for yourself, or do the work in this book.) Write a list of all of the things you can do instead of contacting him or leaning on friends:

_____	_____	_____
_____	_____	_____
_____	_____	_____
_____	_____	_____

Another problem with trying to be "just friends" is that it can keep one person in the relationship in limbo—usually the person who is broken up with. It is not fair to the one who still has feelings to be friends because he or she might stay hooked into the relationship and be prevented from moving on. This is not healthy for either of you. I believe that being best friends can work, and you are the only one who knows your situation. You have to be your own barometer. Just be aware of the negative potential.

> *"If you love somebody, let them go.*
> *If they return, they were always yours.*
> *If they don't, they never were."*
> —Anonymous

If you are supposed to be friends or lovers again it will happen naturally—eventually. If, and when, both of you are in a better place where you have gratitude and love, feel free to be friends (but please be honest with yourself). And don't rush it.

If you are having difficulty moving on and healing, then I suggest DISTANCE. When I say distance I mean giving yourself some time and space away from the other person. This is how we grow and change.

List all of the ways that you are still connected to your ex (i.e., still go to the same gym, shop at the same grocery store, work together, share the same dog, live together, have the same group of friends, have children together, etc.).

_____   _____   _____

_____   _____   _____

_____   _____   _____

_____   _____   _____

Diana T. (continued)

Then one night, after dinner and a movie, it happened. We made love. We were so connected—it was so good. I can't remember the last time we made love like that. He was so attentive to my needs, listened to what I had to say. It was like when we first met. We fell in love all over again...

SEX WITH THE EX?

"Sex with an ex can be depressing. If it's good, you don't have it anymore. If it's bad, you just had sex with an ex."
—Samantha from *Sex in the City*

If you do decide to continue to have sex with your ex, be careful. We love the high feeling, the endorphin rush. Women bond with men through sex, even when we talk ourselves into believing that it is just a meaningless fling. This is because of a sexually stimulated love hormone called oxytocin, which allows a woman to reach orgasm. Once a woman has had sex with a man, she is connected to him. When he is around, her senses are aroused and her body chemistry is thrown off balance, and she is instantly attracted to him again. It's pure biological fact. This is why a lot of women stay with men even when they intellectually know that they are wrong for them. Yes, men also produce oxytocin. However, they are generally less emotionally affected by it. I suggest that you be aware of this and if you do decide to have sex with your ex, take a strong and hard look at how this is serving you in the overall scheme of things.

Sex with an Ex Questionnaire

Have you ever had sex with an ex? [ ] yes no [ ]

List the positives:

_____

_____

_____

List the negatives:

_____

_____

_____

Are you having sex with your ex now? [ ] yes no [ ]

List the positives:

_____

_____

_____

List the negatives:

_____

_____

_____

From a La La Land perspective, what would it be like to continue having sex with your ex?

_____

_____

_____

From a Reality Land perspective, what would it be like to continue having sex with your ex?

_____

_____

_____

Diana T. (continued)

We discussed getting back together for about 2 minutes and then decided we should. It would all be different this time. Our problems of the past would stay in the past. He had changed. I had changed. We had changed.

We renewed our verbal vows and proceeded to begin our relationship anew...

FROM BREAKING UP TO MAKING UP
OR:
HERE YESTERDAY, GONE TOMORROW, HERE AGAIN TODAY

> "What do you do if your boyfriend walks out?
> : Close the door."
> —Anonymous

Don't count on reconciliation working. Most don't. So, you can't count it out. Yes, miracles do happen. You might fall into each other's arms sobbing forgiveness and swearing undying love. You and your ex might work it out. If so, just know that it's going to take a lot of work. He is not going to be perfect. He is still going to be some form of that not so perfect Mr. So & So that you fell in love with the first time around. To make this work both of you will have to come to a full agreement that you are willing to take an honest look at yourself, each other, and your relationship. One thing each of you can do, individually, is write an inventory on:

1. your partner's strengths and weaknesses
2. your strengths and weaknesses
3. the strengths and weaknesses of the relationship

When both of you have completed this exercise, compare what you have written. Talk together until you are comfortable with what the other has written down. Ask yourselves if you are willing to work on those areas that your partner would like you to work on. Finally, negotiate an "I will/I won't" contract (see below). If necessary, you might want to seek professional guidance with a counselor to draw out this contract. In time you will discover whether you are truly meant to be together. But, do realize that people change and you might have to addendumize your contract over time.

Diana T. (continued)

No sooner did it begin again than it began to end again. We did not address the problems of our past—we just metaphorically swept them under the rug. And in the end, once again, they were bigger than our love. THE END.

"I Will—I Won't" Contract

The purpose of this contract is for each of you to commit to working on your undesirable behaviors and qualities. Each of you lists the things you want and don't want the other to do:
I want you to_____ & I don't want you to _____.
   The other person either agrees that he/she will or won't do this:
I will do this or I won't do that. Don't nit pick or make these important issues to the relationship. This is a negotiation process where

both parties have to come to an honest understanding and agreement. When this is achieved, a contract can then be signed. There will still be lots of hard work and issues that must be dealt with. Realize that it is never in your best interest to be somebody you are not just to win the other back. Your true self will eventually come through the cracks.

All that said, not all couples have reconcilable differences. If one, or both, refuses to change, then this contract will be broken and the reconciliation will fail. But your attempt is not a failure, it's a win. If this happens, you now know conclusively that your relationship was not meant to be and you can move forward.

The contract is useful when conflict arises in any relationship, even if it is only one-sided. You can establish your own boundaries.

> *"Breaking-up is hard to do but it's much easier, with the same person, the second time around."*
> —Colette Huemer

FROM "YOUR PLACE OR MINE?" TO OUR PLACE IS OURS. TO A PLACE OF MY OWN—ALONE.

> *"To stand still is to lose, to move is to gain, to change is to grow."*
> —Anonymous

If you live with your ex, I recommend that you make plans for separate living situations—right away. If it's your place, ask him to move out. If it's his place, get out. If the two of you own a place together, you should seek legal advice to keep yourself protected. Whatever you do, don't stay in an unhealthy relationship or hide your head in the sand.

Cohabitation Questionnaire

Are you living with your ex right now? [ ] yes [ ] no

If yes, what are the steps you need to take to live separately? (i.e., move out, get a lawyer, find a new apartment, ask him to move out and get a hotel until he does so, etc.).

_____

_____

_____

_____

I SHAT WHERE I ATE

If you work with him, well, there's no way around it, it's going to be difficult. It will be especially important to keep yourself emotionally balanced through this transition. Each situation has its own challenges. Regardless of your particular situation, I suggest that you distance yourself from him, when you can.

After the break-up you might, for example, want to take some personal days off of work—without jeopardizing your job, that is. Don't bring your baggage to work (remember, it's not a vacation, it's work). Don't talk about your ex at work, even if he talks about you. Water cooler gossip will only cause drama.

Try not to be around him or put yourself in a vulnerable position while at work. If you have to interact with him, be professional. Don't put yourself in social situations where you'll bump into each other. In other words, no more Friday night happy hours with the folks from work. Go out with your other friends instead.

NOTE: If you are being demeaned, sexually harassed, skipped over for a promotion, or feel extremely uncomfortable by or around your ex, you will have to reassess your employment situation and even consider leaving your job. Once again, only you will know what's right in your situation. You are your own barometer.

Work and Love Questionnaire

Are you in a work-love relationship? [ ] yes [ ] no

If yes, what is it like for you to work together and have a simultaneous love relationship?

_____

_____

_____

_____

What are some of the negatives that have come out of this dynamic?

_____

_____

_____

_____

What are some of the positives that have come out of this dynamic?

_____

_____

_____

_____

If you were in a love/work relationship, how was it for you emotionally when it ended? Did you feel uncomfortable, embarrassed, or scared that you would lose your job? Write about your experience.

_____

_____

_____

_____

How did you resolve the situation? Or, have you?

_____

_____

_____

_____

What can you do to empower yourself? (i.e. not go to the same happy hour, not take the same lunch, etc.)

_____

_____

_____

_____

I suggest that you really stick to not doing these things. The only person hurt by not taking your power is you

IF YOU GET THE KIDS, AT LEAST I GET THE DOG

"Most of the damages are done before the divorce. Staying together may not be the best choice, and particularly if kids are living in a household where the parents are always fighting."
—Lisa Strohschein

Children and pets are the number one reason why people stay connected after a break up and/or divorce. Many times one person uses children or pets as an excuse to keep the other person connected. If you have children and/or animals, I suggest that you don't use them as a selfish tool to continue a relationship that is over.

If you have kids, take responsibility and be a model for them. They become what they see. I suggest that you get rid of any unhealthy emotions you have towards your ex for your children's sake. Your relationship not working out is not their fault. Once you work through the remedies and recognize the gifts your ex brought you, focus on them instead of the negative issues. And whatever you do, do not bad mouth your ex in front of your children, it only hurts them now and will hurt you in the long run. The term *broken home* only exists because we break it. When children are involved, it is no longer a matter of you and me, it is we. If there are problems in your situation, I suggest that you seek counseling. There are different options: therapists, individual counseling, and counselors through school and church.

Kids Questionnaire

Do you have children with your ex? [ ] yes [ ] no

What steps can you do to make this transition work for all involved?

_____

_____

_____

_____

_____

If you do have kids, list some things that you can do to make this easier on your kids.

_____

_____

_____

_____

_____

_____

WHEN YOU LEAST EXPECT IT, THERE THEY ARE

"It's a small world after all.
It's a small, small world."
—Sherman Brothers

It's a small world. Any way you cut it, running into an ex is almost always awkward. I suggest that you not stress about what will be some day in the future. It will be what it will be.

It's a Small World Questionnaire

List the places that you frequented together (i.e., you went to the same gym, grocery store, "your" restaurant, bar, etc.):

_____

_____

_____

_____

_____

Is it important for you to continue to frequent these places?
[ ] yes [ ]no

Can you find a new place to call your own? [ ] yes [ ]no

If yes, write a list of some new places you could go instead:

_____

_____

_____

_____

_____

Have you every partaken in a drive-by or shown up where you knew an ex might be? [ ] yes [ ] no

If yes, how did you feel before, during, and after?
Before_____
During_____
After_____

I suggest that you do not go anywhere if you KNOW your ex is going to be there (i.e., If your best friend tells you she heard he was going to the local pub on Saturday night, no matter how much you might want to plan a "chance" run in, don't).

If and when you do run into or decide to see your ex, ask yourself:

What did I learn from the encounter?

_____

_____

_____

_____

How can I grow from this experience?

_____

_____

_____

_____

What do I not want to repeat again?

_____

_____

_____

_____

Now move on. And whatever you do, don't be a stalker.

FRIENDS

"Keep smiling, keep shining,
You can always count on me!
That's what friends are for."
—Carole Bayer Sager

"No matter who broke your heart, or how long it takes to heal,
you'll never get through it without your friends."
—Carrie from *Sex in the City*

Nicole X.

A friend in need is a friend in deed until you and your ex break up. Then it's every man or woman for him/herself. Who likes who more? Were they your friend or his friend? Who wants to be a back stabbing bitch and sleep with your ex?

When my ex and I broke up, I went from a couple dozen "so-called" friends to less than a handful of real friends that I could trust. I guess that sometimes less is more. At least I figured out where I stood with some of these people. Since the BIG break-up, I have been able to reconnect to my real friends. I couldn't have gotten through this without them.

friend_ship_ [**frend**-ship]
-noun
1. the state of being a friend; association as friends: to value a person's friendship.
2. a friendly relation or intimacy.
3. friendly feeling or disposition.
4. companionship

Boo-hoo, boo-hoo, oh woe is me.
Won't someone come out and play with me?

True friendship is an in-depth connection between two people that continues in good times and in bad. It fulfills the needs for both people, as well as showing patience and compromise. In the real world, true friendships are few and far between. There are different types of friends: childhood friends, school friends, best friends, long-distance friends, phone friends, faceless Internet friends with funny screen names, shopping friends, party friends, old friends, and new friends, to name a few. The question is, are they your true friends or just friends in name? Or, are they your Foe?

A friend is a person you can rely on, confide in, and trust. Friends are loyal, honest, see you for who you are, will call you on your s#!t, help you grow, are a mirror reflection of you, make a difference in your life, support you, will tell you when they disagree, say nice things about you, make you feel good about yourself, snap you out of La La Land and back into Reality Land when you need to (or allow you just to be), value you, call you just to say hi, believe in you, give you a shoulder to cry on, and tell you the truth—whatever they do, they do it honestly. Friends give us company, share similar interests, enjoy similar activities, may have the same sense of style and personality, share the same values, and sometimes agree to disagree. Like intimate love relationships, we attract certain friends into our lives to learn more about ourselves. Friendships also require a willingness to work through difficult times, as well as communication. And they take two to tango. All of this can make your friendships truly rewarding.

However you are feeling right now, it is good to have a friend to talk to after your break-up. Friends are there for you to share the feelings that you are having about your ex. Nonetheless, as I said earlier, you do want to be careful not to take advantage of your friends as a listening board. Do not abuse and drain them. If all you do is **talk and**

talk and talk about your ex, they might avoid you and your calls. Be sure to ask their permission if it is all right for you to talk about your ex once more. Try to take contrary action and let them know how you are ready to grow from your experience and not be a victim. Be an example of how you are taking responsibility, becoming more self-aware, and taking care of yourself. And remember to question yourself as to what kind of a friend you are.

Friendship Questionnaire

What kind of a friend are you?

_____

_____

_____

_____

What are five traits that you look for in a friend?

_____

_____

_____

_____

_____

Make a list of your current true friends and what you like about each one:

Friend   What you like about them

_____   _____

_____   _____

_____   _____

_____   _____

Continue free writing on these subjects in YOUR BOOK.

"Friendship? Yes Please."
—Charles Dickens

What To Do When a Third Wheel Becomes a Flat Tire

"Don't be dismayed at goodbyes.
A farewell is before you can meet again.
And meeting again after a moment or a lifetime
is certain for those who are friends."
—Richard Bach

Unfortunately, on one level or another almost all of us lose touch with our friends when we fall in love. You might spend less time with your closest friends, others you might have lost complete touch with. These choices are both conscious and unconscious—some for the right reasons, some for the wrong. Sometimes you become closer to those friends that you can double or triple date with because you enjoy hanging out with other couples when you are one. We might talk ourselves into believing that all of this is okay because it is difficult to do it all—be with a partner, work, exercise, take care of family, have time for yourself, run errands, and then friends (and forget about it if you have kids). Whatever your excuse, in life and love, we do from time to time lose touch with those we once cared about.

There are many reasons why we lose touch with our friends while we are in love relationships. Your friend might not have approved of your lover. She might be jealous because your lover is taking you away from her, or because she is single and doesn't want to relate. Perhaps you talk endlessly about your relationship, and that annoys your friend. You might begin to share less because of privacy issues with your significant other. You and your friend might begin to have different values. You might be so changed by the new lover that you and your friend have less in common. You might be so busy that you choose to spend the little free time you do have with your lover instead of your friend.

Friendships have their ups and downs, and their trials and tribulations. For whatever reason, some are meant to be renewed and some are not. It's up to you to invite someone back into your life or accept their invitation.

Friends Questionnaire

Do any of your friends do the following?:

Only call you when they need something from you? [ ] yes [ ] no

Borrow things from you and not return them? [ ] yes [ ] no

Steal things from you? [ ] yes [ ] no

Talk badly about you or stab you in your back? [ ] yes [ ] no

Say mean things to you on purpose? [ ] yes [ ] no

Ask you for favors and then never reciprocate? [ ] yes [ ] no

Compete with you as if you where their rival? [ ] yes [ ] no

Completely dump you when they are in a relationship? [ ] yes [ ] no

Flirt with your boyfriend or girlfriend when you have one? [ ] yes [ ] no

Show signs that they would steal your lover from you? [ ] yes [ ] no

IF YOU ANSWERED YES TO ANY OF THESE QUESTIONS, YOU HAVE TO ASK YOURSELF IF THIS PERSON IS YOUR FRIEND!!! ASK YOURSELF WHY YOU CHOSE THIS PERSON IN YOUR LIFE AND HOW YOU SHARE THE SAME QUALITIES.

List any friends for which you answered yes to the above questionnaire. For each one, write how they serve you both negatively and positively. What part do you play in this dynamic? Own that. Then decide how you want them to continue to be in your life—or not.

Name: _____

Positives: _____

_____

_____

Negatives: _____

_____

_____

What is your part? _____

_____

_____

What role do you want them to have in your life? _____

_____

_____

How can you change yourself and your dynamic with that person to better improve the relationship?

_____

_____

_____

_____

How can you communicate this to her in a non-combative way?

_____

_____

_____

_____

Do you do any of the following to your friends?:

Only call when you need something? [ ] yes [ ] no

Borrow things and not return them? [ ] yes [ ] no

Steal things? [ ] yes [ ] no

Talk badly about them or stab them in their back? [ ] yes [ ] no

Say mean things to them on purpose? [ ] yes [ ] no

Ask for favors and then never reciprocate? [ ] yes [ ] no

Compete with them as if you where their rival? [ ] yes [ ] no

Completely dump them when you're in a relationship? [ ] yes [ ] no

Flirt with their boyfriends or girlfriends? [ ] yes [ ] no

Steal their lovers? [ ] yes [ ] no

Do you need to make any amends to any of your friends? If so, to whom and why?

_____

_____

_____

_____

Do you want to reconnect with any friends? If so, with whom and why?

_____

_____

_____

_____

Continue free writing on these subjects in YOUR BOOK.

Mutual friends who are no longer mutual
With friends like that, who needs enemies?

Some of the people you and your ex shared as mutual friends might not choose to be in your life anymore. Some of your friends might choose your ex over you. You might feel uncomfortable being around some of your mutual friends because you're unsure where their loyalties lie (with you or your ex). You might also not hang out with certain people as much because you used to hang out as couples. Maybe now you're just a third wheel.

Friend or Foe Questionnaire

Write a list of the mutual friends that you and your ex shared. Next to their name write how that relationship has changed, and what that means to you now and in your future.

Name of friend	How and why your relationship has changed	What the change means to you

What I suggest is that you focus on the friends you have in your life today and the new friends that you will have room for. Allow new friends into your life. Get involved in social activities you enjoy (sports, movies, concerts, museums, meet your neighbors, go to any social meetings, visit new places, travel, learn, take classes, go back to school, etc.).

"It's the friends you can call up at 4 a.m. that matter."
—Marlene Dietrich

Make a list of ten things that you have always wanted to do with your friends and haven't.

Maybe you didn't do them because your ex didn't want you to. Maybe you haven't gotten around to asking your friends to join you.

10 things I want to do with my friends.

1. _____

2. _____

3. _____

4. _____

5. _____

6. _____

7. _____

8. _____

9. _____

10. _____

Now I suggest that you go out and grab a friend and do it!

IN CLOSING

So here you are. You've made it through the been there, done that stage. On a certain level it might be the most difficult time that you will go through. It can be one conflicting time after another—freedom and loneliness. It's getting healthy and then engaging in self-destructive behavior. It could be a one-night stand with a stranger or a late night bootie call with your ex. It could be realizing that the friends you thought you had are no longer there for you; yet those friends that are true are there for you more now than ever before. You may have even rekindled you relationship with your ex—if so, be careful not to find yourself falling into the same traps as before. Whatever your case may be, try not to languish in the extremes. You will hopefully find yourself somewhere in the middle.

THE BREAK

AFRAID

I am afraid:

I am Afraid OF <u>NEVER</u> Being/getting married
I am Afraid that I will <u>never</u> find love again
I am afraid of turning **30** and not being engaged
I am afraid of never having a family of my own
I am afraid that I will gain weight.
I Am afraid that I will get fat when I'm pregnant
I am afraid that I have lost MR Gray forever
I am afraid that I won't get this book published.
I am afraid that I won't travel the world
I am afraid that I will **SMOKE** again.
I am afraid of rats
I am afraid that I will live in my one
— bedroom apt forever
I am afraid that

4

-Verb
1. To interrupt or halt an activity.
-Noun
2. An abrupt or marked change, as in sound or direction, or a brief pause.
3. A chance to improve one's lot, esp. one previously unlooked for.
4. A brief, scheduled interruption of a program.
She said she would take care of it after her 15-minute coffee break.

The Break Stage is a time out while you collect your thoughts and feelings.

How long will it take?...
Are we there yet?...
Are we there yet?...
Are we there yet?...
Are we there yet?...

The break is your break from external distractions, which keep you repeating your same patterns from relationship to relationship. This break can allow you the time to find internal clarity. In a perfect world, this time should be about you, nothing but YOU. But, as we all should know by now—we don't live in a perfect world. La La Land only exists in fairytales. So, use this time wisely. It will take as long as it takes.

Nick T.

It's been three weeks since my break-up and the pain hasn't gone away. I don't know if it ever will. Everything reminds me of the relationship—I mean everything! I can't sleep. I can't eat. My stomach is in knots. Even though I know it's over, I just can't accept it. I want the way I feel to stop. I just don't know how or what to do. If I did, I would do it.

AS LONG AS IT TAKES

"Sometimes I lie awake at night, and I ask,
'Where have I gone wrong?'
Then a voice says to me,
'This is going to take more than one night.'"
—Charlie Brown

Most of us want to know how long the hurt is going to last. Everyone seems to have an answer: 365 days (366 if it's a leap year), 9 months, 6 months, 90 days, 30 days, half the time you were involved in the relationship, 30 minutes or less, or your next relationship is free. Trouble is, none of these time frames takes YOU into consideration. It is up to you to decide how quickly you want to grow and evolve— while waiting for that relationship you always wished for.

Every situation, break-up, and relationship is a unique experience and story. There is no abracadabra, wave a magic wand, "Open Sesame," rub the genie's lamp, make a wish and the heart is healed. Healing is its own process in your own time.

During this time, it's not a good idea to make any rash decisions. Better to ask for advice, sleep on it, and weigh your options. However, if you do take these steps with the intention of healing your heart, it will be healed. Visualization is a key step in this process. The healing will happen. It's happening right now!

If you can see it, you can be it.

If you allow yourself to shift internally, change will happen and you will transform. The trick is to live in the solution, not in the problem.

"They say that time changes things,
but you actually have to change them yourself."
- Andy Warhol

FEAR

"Our deepest fears are like dragons,
guarding our deepest treasure."
—Rainer Maria Rilke

It is okay if you are afraid right now. We have all, at some point in our lives, been afraid of something. For some people it is walking into a party and feeling like a wallflower, for some it is getting out of their comfort zone and traveling to a different country, for some it is riding a scary rollercoaster, for some it is calling a long-lost family member or friend and reconnecting, for some it is the fear of never finding love and feeling alone. I understand that there are reasons for your fears, and it is important for you to honor them. However, for your own growth you will want to find out where your fears stem from, and then face them. They may stem from an early childhood experience or an old, instilled belief. Whatever your reasons, they are there, and it's important to trace them to their roots. Fear paralyzes us from reaching our full potential.

Fear can make us believe that we are losing instead of gaining. It allows us to live in the negative instead of the positive and gives us more pain than pleasure. Fortunately, it is entirely possible to diminish, even banish our fears. But it does take some work.

"*The only thing we have to fear is fear itself.*"
—Franklin D. Roosevelt

Your Fear Inventory

Write a list of all of the things that you are afraid of. Keep writing your fears until you can no longer write any more.

I am afraid of_____

I am afraid of_____

I am afraid of_____

I am afraid of_____

I am afraid of_____

I am afraid of_____

I am afraid of_____

I am afraid of_____

I am afraid of_____

I am afraid of_____

I am afraid of_____

I am afraid of_____

I suggest that you read your inventory out loud to somebody you trust.

Are your fears something that you can overcome? [ ] yes [ ] no

This time there is only one correct answer and it is YES. You CAN overcome your fears.

A good way of beginning to get over your emotional fears is by first challenging yourself to get over a physical fear, because once you experience getting through a physical fear, you will discover that you can work through your emotional fears as well. The physical challenge is not a cure-all, but it lets you know what you are capable of.

It is a symbol of your willingness to overcome your emotional fears in everyday life.

Now pick a physical fear of yours and face it.

DISCLAIMER: DO WITH CAUTION. DO NOT DO ANYTHING OVERLY DANGEROUS OR ILLEGAL THAT COULD CAUSE PHYSICAL HARM OR INCARCERATION!!!

VICTIM OR NOBODY'S FOOL
WHY ME? WHY THIS? WHY THAT? WHY NOT?
WHY? WHY? WHY? WHY? WHY?

"Nobody can hurt me without my permission."
—Mahatma Gandhi

Oftentimes when we look at why our relationships end, we focus on our victimization. We project, blame, and tend not to take responsibility for our own choices. There are many different reasons why you would naturally feel victimized when experiencing emotional anguish after a lost love relationship. All of your dreams and fantasies about your future with this person are now shattered. Everything you had envisioned has faded.

You may be feeling the pressure to be in a relationship from your family, friends, and society. As a female you may feel the pressures of your biological clock ticking. As a male you might feel the urgency to carry on your lineage. You may be going through or have gone through a divorce and not know where you are heading. You may not want to marry or have a family; you may simply yearn for a partnership and affection. Whatever your reason is, you feel loss. That is to be expected. That is normal.

Will G.

I never should have let her move in. I never should have let her leave a toothbrush in the cup on my sink. Once I did, the relationship was all downhill. Nothing was ever enough. First it was this. Then it was that. Once she got her way one way, she would find something else to complain about. It wasn't all her fault. 99.9% of it was me—who I was that she didn't like and wanted to change.

THE BLAME GAME

> *"The best day of your life is the one on which you decide your life is your own. No apologies or excuses. No one to lean on, rely on, or **blame**. The gift is yours— it is an amazing journey—and you alone are responsible for the quality of it. This is the day your life really begins."*
> —Bob Moawad

The truth is that everyone sometime, somewhere, somehow has had a break-up in which they felt like a victim. You find yourself asking, "How could I have been so in love and the relationship not work out?" You may even be saying, "I can't believe he did this to me. I deserve better. How dare he?" Or, "What am I going to do? I can't live without her." "I'm lonely. I'm depressed. I'm _____ . I don't know what to do." "I did nothing wrong. I'm the victim here!" He did this; she did that...blah blah blah.

But you know what? Blaming takes a lot of time and energy. It distracts you from keeping the focus on yourself, which is what you need to be doing right now. Don't play the blame game. It's time to look at your own part. After all, you're the only one you can do anything about anyway, right?

The Blame Questionnaire

Do you blame other people, circumstances, the times, social pressures, prejudice, or bad timing for what you consider to be mistakes or failures? [ ] yes [ ] no

Do you feel cheated or shortchanged? [ ] yes [ ] no

If yes, list how:

_____

_____

_____

_____

List three things that you need to do but have been avoiding since your break-up.

_____

_____

_____

What are some of the obstacles standing in your way?

_____

_____

_____

_____

What can you do to remove these obstacles and follow through with these things? (Formulate a game plan.)

_____

_____

_____

_____

What do you think your ex did to you to make you a victim?

_____

_____

_____

_____

What is the greatest pain that your partner caused you?

_____

_____

_____

_____

Was there any verbal, physical, or emotional abuse? [ ] yes [ ] no

If yes, how often did this happen?_____

If yes, why did you tolerate the abuse?

_____

_____

_____

_____

Can you own your part in this dynamic and realize that you are not the victim? [ ] yes [ ] no

If yes, write down your part. If no, keep looking within yourself until you can.

_____

_____

_____

_____

Continue free writing on these subjects in YOUR BOOK.

Look, this is your party and you can cry if you want to. You can sit in your room and eat bon bons for months, listen to sad love songs, go out and have 100 one-night stands, drink a case of beer, etc...basically self-destruct. You can say, "I can't, I'm not good enough, this isn't fair, I never could..." It is your choice.

But no matter what your ex did to you, how much fault you see in him, or how much you despise him, it is a waste of your time and energy to blame him. If you feel like expressing to your ex how much he betrayed you or hurt you, it might make him feel bad for a moment, but it will not change him. If his actions are upsetting you, it's time to ask yourself what it is in **you** that is making you upset. What can you change within **yourself?**

Fool me once shame on you.
Fool me twice shame on me.
Fool me thrice...

"I must learn to **love** *the* **fool** *in me—the one who feels too much, talks too much, takes too many chances, wins sometimes and loses often, lacks self-control, loves and hates, hurts and gets hurt, promises and breaks promises, laughs and cries."*
—Theodore Isaac Rubin

We are only victims when we are out of control of our own lives. Victims operate from weakness. A victim might feel that she is *forced* to spend time with family members she doesn't like, be responsible for everyone else's well being, that he has to pay for everyone, that she is there for everyone but herself and taking care of everyone else's problems. When you are a victim, you are still living in your past story and childhood experiences—of your alcoholic or chronically fighting or overly authoritarian parents, your abusive step-father, etc. And it may well be that you did not get your emotional needs met. But that story is in the past. It's not your truth anymore.

Victim Questionnaire

Where do you feel you have been victimized in this world (childhood, family, friends, job)?

_____

_____

_____

_____

_____

_____

_____

How did that make you feel at the time?

_____

_____

_____

_____

_____

_____

_____

_____

How does it make you feel today?

_____

_____

_____

_____

_____

_____

_____

_____

If you still believe that you are a victim today, you still have work to do. If you don't get through those experiences and make peace with them, you will continue to feel hurt, angry, lonely, and afraid. When you are a victim, you can't help yourself and you can't grow from the experience. It is this simple: If you focus on the pain and being a victim—you will be in pain and be a victim. You stay in the victim role for one reason: It is your avoidance of growth.

Sometimes we choose to repeat, repeat, and repeat the same behaviors and patterns that do not serve us. We know that we want to be better, but we continue to repeat all the same. We do this because we would much rather stay in the discomfort and drama of our current situation than move on. But remember this: It's **always** up to YOU.

Resentment Inventory

The next time (or any time) you feel like a victim, confront yourself on what your part is. It is also important for you to get over anything that you are angry with yourself for. If you don't let go, you will not be able to move on.

The following exercise, the Resentment Inventory, can help you in letting go. In this resentment inventory:

    1. State the person you resent. Include yourself in situations you resent yourself for.
    2. State what you resent the person (or yourself) for.
    3. State what areas in your life it affected (your financial, physical/health, living environment, family, friendships, personal growth, career, romantic relationship, etc.).
    4. State what your part in the situation was.

Write all of your resentments down. Continue to do this resentment inventory whenever you find yourself resenting someone in your life—past or present.

I resent	For	It affected my	My part was

Continue free writing on these subjects in YOUR BOOK.

Sam L.

My therapist suggested that I look into getting on anti-depressants. I told her no way—there has to be another way of getting out of this hell hole than popping some pill that is going to be a temporary fix. I'm not saying that they don't work—I just want to find another way. I'm just not sure if I should take them or not take them. But, I feel awful. I sleep all day, overeating my sorrows, and can't seem to get my fat ass to the gym. The end of my tunnel is black. My boyfriend breaking up with me has really shook up what I thought my life was going to look like. I'm depressed.

de·pres·sion [di-**presh**-*uhn*]
-noun
1. the state of being depressed.
2. sadness; gloom; dejection.
3. *Psychiatry.* a condition of general emotional dejection and withdrawal; sadness greater and more prolonged than that warranted by any objective reason.

NOBODY'S FOOL
OR:
HOW I KICKED MY VICTIM TO THE CURB

"Never be bullied into silence. Never allow yourself to be made a **victim***. Accept* **no** *one's definition of your life; define yourself."*
—Harvey Fierstein

So, you are not in a relationship right now. In your previous relationship the two of you didn't work out. You may begin to feel like you are in a frustrating and losing battle. You might even begin to believe that relationships are unfair, unsatisfying, and that you do not get a fair chance in love. When a relationship ends, many tend to have a knee-jerk reaction of refusing to love or trust. You may attempt to harden yourself, or keep new relationships superficial. This only keeps you imprisoned in your emotional walls of self-protection. There is little growth in this experience of being the victim.

So, what can you do to prevent yourself from being a victim, from repeating the same patterns, interacting in the same circles, and attracting the same situations?

The antonym for victim is genius, wise man, nobody's fool. I encourage you to find a way to believe that your higher self and all of your agonizing experiences are lessons and gifts to allow you to ultimately grow into the best person you can imagine through its lessons and gifts. If you can find a way to do this, then you will set yourself free.

> The only thing that gets in your way of your
> goals or becoming who you want to be is YOU.

It's time to create new habits and ways of thinking. You may feel a bit weary about this right now; it might take some practice. Whenever you're feeling defeated or hopeless, try saying this to yourself: "Maybe today will be the day that I move past feeling like a victim, angry, weak, and in fear. Maybe today will be the day that I move into forgiveness, strength, and the willingness to receive the gifts from my experience."

No Victim Questionnaire

If you feel like people are standing in your way or that you are short changed, or cheated, why do you suppose you permit this to go on?

_____

_____

_____

Can you find the strength and courage to move on from being a victim? [ ] yes [ ] no

If yes, where is that strength within you? What does it look like?

_____

_____

_____

If you answered no and still feel helpless, then your biggest obsta-

cle is yourself and your attitude—not others. Find a way to take ownership of your life and move past victimhood.

Here are some affirmations you can use to help let go of victim thought patterns. Say them until you believe them, even if that means ten to twenty times a day. You can put them on your fridge, computer, bathroom mirror, wallet, YOUR BOOK, etc.

- I am responsible for when I feel like a victim.
- I let my victim thoughts go.
- I am beautiful, healthy, and whole as I am.
- I am brilliant.
- I am responsible for myself.

The sometimes harsh truth is, your relationship was not supposed to last longer than it did—otherwise you would still be together. When you decide not to be a victim, you will see that the relationship happened—and ended—to teach you some life lessons that you were supposed to learn. When you choose to stop being a victim, you discover how much you can grow from your experience. You see, there is no such thing as a victim (at least not in adulthood and not in relationships). We are, all of us, creators of our own experiences, situations, and thoughts. If you can truly believe, understand, and know this, you will find transformation.

BECOME FREE! It is up to you.

> *"Let us resolve to be masters, not the victims,*
> *of our history, controlling our own destiny without*
> *giving way to blind suspicions and emotions."*
> —John Fitzgerald Kennedy

RELEASE

re_lease_ [ri-**lees**]
1. to free from confinement, bondage, obligation, pain, etc.; to let go.
2. to free from anything that restrains, fastens, etc.
3. to allow to be known, issued, done, or exhibited.
4. to give up, relinquish, or surrender (a right, claim, etc.).

Releasing, letting go of something that holds you back or confines you, is an important part of the growth process that break-ups offer us. When we hold onto toxic things, people, behaviors, energies, and resentments, we can't move forward. But we can't just magically let go, either. We have to let ourselves feel whatever we are feeling, move through it and then move on.

Release Inventory

What are you trying to release in you or about you? What will hold you back from doing this work on yourself? Your fears, pains, frustrations, control, addictions, self-destructive behaviors, certain family members or friends?

As you realize what or whom it is you are trying to release, write it down and acknowledge it:

_____	_____	_____
_____	_____	_____
_____	_____	_____
_____	_____	_____
_____	_____	_____
_____	_____	_____
_____	_____	_____

One of the keys to releasing yourself from the past, not to mention creating healthy relationships, lies in setting good boundaries. If you start by setting boundaries with the old, you also begin to train yourself for healthier boundaries in the new. When you let go of old things that no longer serve you, you allow room for the new.

The Box Exercise
Or:
The Container, The Brown Paper Bag, The Envelope, The Tupperware, The Ziploc Bag

The Box is a private place, shoebox, bag, envelope, etc. that belongs only to you. Write down your worries, fears, questions, angers, frustrations, and anything that is out of your control and put them in your box. If you have doubts, confusions, fear over relationships, money, jobs, friends, etc, write the issue down, place it in The Box. You can place pictures of the two of you, old love letters and poems in there. By placing them in The Box you can release your concerns and turn them over because they are out of your control.

Mark K.

Hindsight is 20-20. When my ex and I first broke up I thought she was crazy for saying that I needed to change some things about myself. Looking back, she was right about a few things. There were some things in me that on reflection I needed to change and did. It was hard for me to look at these things when we were wrapped up in our mess. I had to take a step back to see things more clearly. There are moments when I regret acting the way I did. But, there is nothing I can do to change the past. I have to move forward and not repeat those same things. Knowing this has helped me do so.

Your Break Essay
It's not a break down, it's a break up.
Or:
How I took a lemon and made lemonade.

Now that you have read about victimization, write your story, focusing on the positives that your relationship brought you. This will be a step in taking you from Victimhood to Nobody's Fool.

    Once upon a time... (Insert your story here.)

_____

_____

_____

_____

_____

_____

_____

_____

_____

_____

_____

_____

_____

_____

_____

_____

_____

_____

_____

Continue free writing on these subjects in YOUR BOOK.

DISTRACTION
SPENDING TIME ALONE WITH ME, MYSELF, AND I

"There is only one journey. Going inside yourself."
—Rainer Maria Rilke

Do you crave spending time alone or avoid it? [ ] Crave it [ ] Avoid it

Your alarm clock awakens you at 6am so that you can get to the office by 8am, bumper-to-bumper traffic, endless errands to run, cell phones ringing, text messages in your inbox, phone calls to return, faxes coming in, emails to write and respond to, back-to-back meetings at work, hardly a moment to eat a healthy meal at lunchtime, dinner meetings and functions to attend, weekends filled with friends, dinner parties, birthdays, weddings, and catching up to do, the next holiday to plan for, and by the time evening rolls around, it's grabbing something quick and easy to eat, crashing your head against the pillow, hoping for a good night's rest, so you can get up the next day and do it all again. Distraction. Distraction. Distraction.

Realistically, all activities have to come to an end and we all must come back to our "me, myself, and I." That can be tough because we often involve ourselves in activities in order to avoid being alone with our hurts and realities. Once again, you have a choice: you can deal with yourself in your conscious waking state or you will be dealing with yourself in your restless sleep (nightmares). One way or another, you will deal with yourself. POINT BLANK, THIS IS THE LIFE THAT YOU HAVE CREATED FOR YOURSELF. Deal with it.

BEING ALONE
A NECESSARY EVIL OR HOW I SPEND MY MONEY AT THE MALL

*"We are so obsessed with doing that we have no time
and no imagination left for being."*
—Thomas Merton

It's time to get comfortable with being alone. Many people ask the question, "Why do I need to spend time alone?" The answer is simple: because it is essential for your growth and well being. We all need time to reflect—on our lives, our day, how our emotions are affecting our outlook, our treatment of others, how we are feeling—and to engage in solo activities that we enjoy. Being alone gives us a chance to focus on who we are as individuals.

NOTE: Some people end up spending too much time alone, as a way of avoiding the world around them. If you are someone who tends to withdraw, be careful about spending too much time alone. Being a hermit is not healthy either. It's all a matter of balance.

Too often in love relationships we give up our individuality. This can be the time for you to reclaim yours. Now that your relationship is over, take advantage of this alone time. Reevaluate what you like to do. You do not have to be afraid of this. Embrace it.

If you are uncomfortable with spending time by yourself, you might want to start off with short spans of time. You might begin with having a quiet cup of tea or coffee in the morning, or take walks by yourself. I am not suggesting that you run out and join a monastery. However, you might be pleasantly surprised at the things that come to you when you spend time with yourself. This is when you can create an opportunity to go within yourself and acknowledge even more about the choices you have made and change your old patterns.

Spending time alone, by the way, does not mean that you have to be serious. Have fun with you! Celebrate yourself and what you enjoy.

There are many ways to take care of your mind, body and spirit. By experimenting, you can open new doors to creativity and your beauty. You don't have to be shy about doing some external changes either. Be creative with your outer beauty. We all need to do this at times. Express your external self in whatever way fits you (as long as it's safe and legal!). It is perfectly wonderful to pamper yourself, just as long as you remember that the external will not fix the internal.

I'm free to do anything I want any time, anywhere, anyhow.

Write down your Top Ten List of things to do alone: (ex. Find an intention for your life, pamper yourself with a day at the spa, take long walks, go to the gym, take a yoga class or watch a yoga DVD and try it at home, ride that bike that has been sitting in your garage for years, travel, go to the movies, go shopping, read a book, take a nap, rent some old movies, meditate).

1. _____
2. _____
3. _____
4. _____
5. _____
6. _____
7. _____
8. _____
9. _____
10. _____

NOTE: After you do these things write down how they affect you both positively and/or negatively. Then decide which ones serve you the best in your life in this moment.

The Think It Over Questionnaire

What does spending time alone feel like to you?

_____

_____

_____

_____

_____

Do you love it or hate it? [ ] love it [ ] hate it

Do you look forward to it or avoid it? [ ] look forward to it [ ] avoid it

How often do you spend time alone? [ ] never [ ] seldom [ ] frequently [ ] always

Do you want to start spending more time alone? [ ] yes [ ] no

If no, why? What would you rather be doing with your time?

_____

_____

_____

_____

If yes, what would you like to start doing in your extra alone time?

_____

_____

_____

_____

Many times when we are in a love relationship we stop doing the things we enjoy because our lover doesn't enjoy them, we're embarrassed by what we enjoy, or we're afraid that we will be judged. We focus so much on the relationship that we forget about the things that we love, or we simply stop doing them.

What are the top ten things that you stopped doing because of your ex?

The Top 10 Things I Stopped Doing Because of My Ex:

1. _____

2. _____

3. _____

4. _____

5. _____

6. _____

7. _____

8. _____

9. _____

10. _____

CLEANSE YOUR ENVIRONMENT
SPRING-CLEANING DOES NOT JUST HAVE TO COME ONCE A YEAR. SOMETIMES RELATIONSHIPS FAIL IN THE FALL.

Next to the actual moment of a break-up, cleaning up the aftermath can be the most difficult part of the transition period. The aftermath can be remnants of the relationship, an old pair of blue jeans, a borrowed television set, unpaid bills that you shared, a half eaten box of their cereal, and photos, photos and more photos. What are you going to do? Sleep with those blue jeans under your pillow? Even watching that television, no matter what program is on, will remind you of him. It's time to move on.

It doesn't matter if it's spring, summer, fall, or winter—there is no better time than now to do your "spring" cleaning. Throw away that box of cereal. Pay your bills. (No matter how you deal with them, you don't want them to go to collection agencies.) Return the television, and if he doesn't want it, give it to Goodwill. Goodwill will even pick it up from your residence. Pack up the things that remind you of your ex. Just like you need space from him for a while, you need space from the things of his that occupy your physical environment. By all means don't torture yourself by keeping his things around in hopes of winning him back. You might want to take down all the pictures of the two of you for the time being. If you want to keep them, put them in a safe place for a later date. I'm not suggesting that you impulsively bury and erase your memories. True closure involves coming face to face with all parts of the relationship—the good, the bad, and the pretty ugly—and immersing yourself in your inner experience of it.

Scrub a dub dub, Spic and Span.
If I can't have Mr. Right then at least I can have Mr. Clean.

Now that you've cleansed remnants of him out of your life, it's time for you to clean up your own mess. Your environment impacts your well-being, state of mind, and health. There is a lot to be said for clearing out the old and allowing room for the new. You get to purify any remaining negativity you may feel and create a new beginning with a renewed attitude of positivity.

Since you might have spent a lot of time with your ex in your bedroom, it might be a good idea to focus on this area. Maybe it's time to paint your bedroom a new color, change your furniture around, put new pictures on your walls, get a new mattress, or take your old bed sheets and donate them to Goodwill.

Are you a pack rat? Have you been collecting and collecting over the years? Do you have any old clothes that you can donate to charity? Do you have any broken things that need to be fixed, and any light bulbs that need to be changed?

By clearing out and reorganizing your environment, you can create a sense of inner clarity and stability, which allows you room for a fresh and clean start. Cleaning out the old will allow room for the new.

Take 5

With all of this work that you are doing on yourself, don't forget to take five and have some fun. Eat some chocolate, sing out loud in your car, dance a silly dance or just meditate.

List 10 things that you love to do but haven't been doing lately:

1. _____

2. _____

3. _____

4. _____

5. _____

6. _____

7. _____

8. _____

9. _____

10. _____

Now schedule them in your day planner or calendar, and just do them.

> *"All work and no play makes Jack a dull boy.*
> *All work and no play makes Jack a dull boy.*
> *All work and no play makes Jack a dull boy.*
> *All work and no..."*
> —Stephen King

IN CLOSING

How long is it going to take? That's up to you. We each have to decide how important things are to us to determine how much time we allot to them. The more time you spend, the more quickly you will get through this stage of your break-up. The only thing you have to fear is fear of yourself. You're not a victim unless you allow yourself to be. The only loser in the blame game is you. So, release those fears, anxiety, overwhelming feelings, and uncontrollable outcomes and make a plan for yourself to move forward. Being alone is not the end of the world, it's your chance to see your world without all the distractions clouding your vision.

THE BREAK IN

Dear Little Eris,

I am so sorry that you are hurting right now. I understand that you feel scared and alone. But I want for you to know that you have me and that I love you. I **REALLY** do understand how you feel and that it is not your fault.

    I need for you to talk to me - tell me when you are afraid and how you are feeling. I will do my best to protect you from those situations. I can't be perfect - but I'll do my best. I will listen more. I will do my b[est] the mother you always wan[ted and] needed - Today. I Love y[ou]

FROM, BIG ERIS

5

-Phrasal Verb

1. To train or adapt for a purpose.
2. To begin an activity or undertaking. To interrupt a conversation or discussion.
3. To discover the system, key, method, etc.
4. To loosen or soften with use to become easier.

These new shoes are killing me. But I know sooner or later I'll break them in.

The Break In stage is when a person goes on an internal quest to learn from their relationship and grow.

Abracadabra. Hocus Pocus. Open Myself, Sesame.

The Break In is your opportunity to go deep within yourself to discover things about you that you might not have been aware of—at least consciously. It might not be the simplest thing in the world. It can even seem difficult at times to face yourself in the mirror, but it can be a great opportunity to communicate with that other part of you—the unconscious inner child who really wants to be heard and if listened to can help you better understand you. As you discover new aspects of yourself and bring them into your everyday life, you can empower yourself to take control of situations you previously might have been afraid to.

Susan K.

Since my relationship ended, I've been taking a hard look at myself and my past relationships and my parents' relationship. Their dynamic was unhealthy. They fought constantly and were emotionally unavailable to me and my sister—even before they were divorced. I now see these patterns reoccurring in my love relationships. The repetitive fight, make-up, and then fight again. I get so emotionally drained that the other relationships in my life suffer. I always told myself that I would never be in a relationship like my parents'. And, now here I am. Thank God I don't have children.

INNER CHILD

"Goo Goo Gaa Gaa Eek Oop Ork Ahh Ahh." That means I love you.

> *"The most important muse of all is our own inner child."*
> —Stephen Machmanovitch

inner child

noun

1. one's original self that revels in play; also called *child within*

2. the childlike aspect of a person's psyche, esp. when viewed as an independent entity.

Who? What? When? Where? How?
Who am I? What am I? Where am I?

It may sound cliché by now, but each of us really is being held back by an inner child—that childlike aspect in the psyche, the child within. This inner child holds onto old childhood issues and responds to new situations from very old emotions. Your inner child has the beliefs, attitudes, and hurts that you picked up energetically about yourself when you were young. These are illusions that have tremendous powers over your life. This is how your life patterns began.

Your inner child is the voice in you that keeps choosing the same relationships. It does not know any better, and it's your job to teach it. It is the part of you that acts out and allows the drama into your life. It is screaming for love and affection from you. In fact, it has been your whole life. It's saying, "Look at me. Love me." I suggest that you listen to it.

Knowing your personal childhood story might help you understand why your inner child acts out in certain ways one time and different ways another. The little child in us feels afraid, unlovable and alone because our parents consciously or unconsciously emotionally scarred us as they had been scarred. These scars need to be tended to so that your patterns can be stopped. Only with an awareness of your family history and childhood can you stop the patterns that your psyche formed in early childhood.

NURTURE OR NATURE?

"Nothing has a stronger influence psychologically on their environment and especially on their children than the unlived life of the parent."
—C.G. Jung

Where It Might Have Begun

What I'm talking about here is recognizing where your pains began. However, be very aware that blaming everything on your parents, and continuing to do so, does not encourage internal growth. It stunts it.

Whether we were raised by our biological parents or not, we are all affected by those who raised us. Parents—no matter how conscious they are—transmit themselves onto their children. There is no perfect parent, and there is no possible way that a parent can meet all of a child's wants and needs. However, there is a universal problem in that their own mothers and fathers were wounded by their mothers and fathers. From generation to generation both mothers and fathers keep passing their wounds onto their kids.

> *"No man is an island, entire of itself;*
> *every man is a piece of the continent."*
> —John Donne

The next part of your healing process is to put aside any blame and false idealization of your parents and begin to work with the wounds you have acknowledged. I believe that you should know your issues. If you choose to live in them, you will probably feel trapped. Why not free yourself from focusing on being victimized?

Just like in life, you can't change the weather, the fact that tax season rolls around every year, your age, that you have to go to the bathroom, traffic situations, or when your phone is going to ring. Coulda, Shoulda, Woulda...There is nothing that you can do to change your past. Everything that has happened is done. All that you can do is learn more about your past, acknowledge it, and know that all of your past experiences and behaviors are a part of you.

You can't change your past, but you can take charge of yourself and how you react in certain situations, and change your behaviors today. Become aware of your place of wounding and turn painful experiences into teachers to your heart. No, there is no magical formula to make your childhood hurts and traumas go away. But if you give attention to your feelings of pain, hurt, fear, anger, or whatever it may be, and not wallow in them, your feelings will stop taking control of your life. They may continue to show up in your life, but they will no longer be the boss of you.

Your wounds, no matter how painful they are, create who you are, and give you depth. What was not efficiently given to you by your parents, you must give to yourself. If you undertake this task honestly, you will not only experience growth but a different way of experiencing relationships. One of the greatest challenges is to reconcile with your parents, even if it is not with them directly. If you reconcile with your parents, you reconcile with yourself.

THE MOTHER
MOMMY DEAREST VERSUS MAMA MIA
POSTPARTUM DEPRESSION CAN LAST A LIFETIME

Unfortunately, motherhood is so difficult that nobody could possibly do it perfectly. But, it's perfect in its own imperfection. A mother/child relationship is complicated, and powerful. Some mothers enjoy the responsibilities that motherhood creates, while others become angry about losing their independence. Whether you have a close and nurturing or terrible and vacant relationship with your mom, you have issues to face that are playing out in your love relationships regarding intimacy. These are issues that are ingrained within and need to be faced to evolve and to become authentically intimate in any interpersonal relationship.

The way a girl's mother was towards her husband and/or the different men in her life will be the girl's example of how to behave, be treated, and treat the men in her life later on. Whereas a boy will learn how to treat women in his life by watching how his mother allows herself to be treated, and how dad did it. If a mother tolerated a dysfunctional relationship with her husband, or vice versa, the child is more likely to tolerate a dysfunctional relationship, or be the one who creates one, in their future relationships.

When there are conflicts in a parent's relationship, instead of communicating amongst themselves, they often seek to meet their needs from their children. The mother may substitute motherhood for friendship. The child may sympathize with her mother and become her protector from the "bad" husband. Alternately, if a father feels unloved by his wife, he may displace his affections onto his children.

A mother-child relationship goes beyond words, no matter what the circumstance. You might have had a relationship with your mother that goes beyond the worst words. You might have been abused, abandoned, lost your mother to an illness, or maybe you never had a mother. If you experience yourself not being able to get past your mother wounds on your own, I suggest that you seek professional help. Nonetheless, I also suggest that you do not stay stuck in your hurt for years and years and years of therapy. At some point you need to move on. That takes courage and strength.

Men who did not get positive attention from their moms usually look for it in their relationships with women. The relationships they had with their mothers usually mirror their expectations of how a woman should act towards them and how they will be with women. Men often choose women who are just like their mommy. If there are mother wounds in the man, he will attract a mate who will trigger those wounds and mirror the unmet needs of that first relationship.

Sometimes men choose women who are the opposite of their mothers. This does not mean that they are necessarily good for them. They might do this as a reaction or a pattern of still reacting to mommy. When a man has internal wounds due to an unhealthy relationship with his mother, he continues to attract unhealthy women who trigger those wounds. A man who had a mother who was absent altogether may go from relationship to relationship—repeatedly looking for love. He continues to look for the Madonna.

The point here is not to blame your mother (or his!) for all of your life's problems. You can't just forgive and forget the past either. But, you can learn to make peace with your mother and understand that she did the best she could do or what felt right to her, given her circumstances, and what was passed onto her from the generations before.

Now that you are older, you can begin to understand her better. If you can be aware of the things that influenced you from your mom, you can begin to change those things within yourself. If you find yourself enmeshed with your mom, it is probably time for you to separate emotionally from her and become your own person. This does not mean that you have to love your mother any less. It just means that you become more of an individual and less enmeshed with her.

You're as American as Mom's Apple Pie

Mother Awareness Questionnaire

This next questionnaire will expose some of your feelings about your mother. If your mother is no longer alive, answer the questions in present day, how you feel right now. If you do not know your biological mother, you can answer the questions about the woman or parent who raised you. Feel free to write whatever comes up for you.

What feelings did you get when thinking about your mother? (Happy feeling, Unhappy feeling, Warm, Cold, Fulfilled, Empty, Loved, Unloved, Controlled, Supported, Understood, Misunderstood, etc.)

_____

_____

_____

Name three things that you like about your mother.

_____

_____

_____

Do you see these things in yourself? List them. How can you utilize these traits in your everyday life?

_____

_____

_____

Name three things that you dislike about your mother.

_____

_____

_____

Do you see these traits in yourself? List them. What can you do to not utilize these traits in your everyday life?

_____

_____

_____

Did your mom ever tell you that she loved you when you were a child? [ ] yes [ ] no

Does your mother tell you that she loves you today? [ ] yes [ ] no

Do you tell your mom that you love her? [ ] yes [ ] no

Do you hold any anger or resentment toward your mom? If so, explain:

_____

_____

_____

Which of your mother's worst traits do you duplicate?

_____

_____

_____

Do you see yourself having the same behaviors and/or patterns as your mother in relationships? Do you have a similar story?

_____

_____

_____

_____

_____

Do you find yourself being attracted to partners who have the same behaviors and/or patterns as your mother? Explain:

_____

_____

_____

_____

The Apple doesn't fall too far from the tree

Mother Essay

Write about any patterns, examples, behaviors, traits, etc. from your mother that you duplicated and brought into your last relationship? How did it/they affect you and your relationship?

_____

_____

_____

_____

_____

_____

_____

_____

_____

_____

_____

_____

_____

_____

_____

_____

_____

_____

_____

_____

_____

_____

_____

_____

_____

_____

_____

_____

_____

_____

If you find yourself still angry at your mother, or any aspect of your relationship (past or present), write an angry letter following the same format as in Chapter 2.

Dear Mom,

_____

_____

_____

_____

_____

_____

_____

_____

_____

Continue free writing on these subjects in YOUR BOOK.

THE FATHER
POTATOE/POTATO—TOMATOE/TOMATO.
IT'S APPLES AND ORANGES,
AND THE APPLE
DOESN'T FALL TOO FAR FROM THE TREE.

A mother is not the only significant relationship in a child's life. It is also important to focus on the father/child relationship. I'm talking about any father figure in your life, be he your biological father, stepfather, grandfather, adoptive father, uncle, etc.

A child's first impression about men comes from their early childhood experiences with their father, or lack thereof. From their fathers, girls form their opinion of what men are and how they should or shouldn't be. A father/son relationship forms the son's identity as a man. Your father may have been present, absent, perfect, abusive or passive. The point is, even if he did everything in his power to be the perfect dad, it is impossible for any one man to fulfill all of his child's wants and desires. Because of this, wounds are created in the psyche. These wounds may not be inflicted with intent, but they do affect us throughout our lives.

Women who did not get positive attention from their dad usually look for it in their relationships with men. The relationships they had with their fathers usually mirror their expectations of how a man should act towards them and how they will be with men.

Women often choose men who are just like their daddy. If there are father wounds in the woman, she will attract a mate who will trigger those wounds and mirror the unmet needs of that first relationship.

Sometimes women choose men who are just the opposite of their fathers. This does not mean that these men are necessarily good for them. They might do this as a reaction or a pattern of still reacting to daddy. When a woman has internal wounds due to an unhealthy relationship with her father, she continues to attract unhealthy men that trigger those wounds.

A woman whose father was absent altogether might create a fantasy-like father in her imagination. Due to her confusion over what a loving partner and human love relationship should look like, she continues to live in a fantasy. She continues to attract men who do not mirror her healthy self. She continues to wish for a savior, projecting that unrealized father fantasy onto the men with whom she becomes intimate.

It is important to know that you can survive in the world without the dependence on your father, his approval, or a father figure. When a woman becomes aware of the relationship of the first male influence in her life, she has a better chance of having a healthy relationship with the masculine. She will learn to set boundaries. Until a woman heals her father wound she will attract her father-like energy in her life.

The way a boy's father was towards his wife and/or the different women in his life will serve as the boy's example of how to behave, be treated, and treat the women in his life later on. A father is a boy's first example of how to be a man. If he is unconscious of this he will often become his father.

You're the Apple of His Eye

Father Awareness Questionnaire

Next is a questionnaire that will expose some of your feelings about your father. If your father is no longer alive, answer the questions in present day, how you feel right now. If you do not know your biological father, you can answer the questions about the man who raised you. Feel free to write whatever comes up for you.

What feelings did you get when thinking about your father? (Happy feeling, Unhappy feeling, Warm, Cold, Fulfilled, Empty, Loved, Unloved, Controlled, Supported, Understood, Misunderstood)

_____

_____

_____

Name three things that you like about your father.

_____

_____

_____

Do you see these things in yourself? List them. How can you utilize these traits in your everyday life?

_____

_____

_____

Name three things that you dislike about your father.

_____

_____

_____

Do you see these traits in yourself? List them. What can you do to not utilize these traits in your everyday life?

_____

_____

_____

Did your dad ever tell you that he loved you when you were a child?
[ ] yes [ ] no

Does your father tell you that he loves you today? [ ] yes [ ] no

Do you tell your dad that you love him? [ ] yes [ ] no

Do you hold any anger or resentment toward your dad? If so,
explain:

_____

_____

_____

Which one of your father's worst traits do you duplicate?

_____

_____

_____

Do you find yourself attracted to partners who have the same
behaviors and patterns as your father? Explain:

_____

_____

_____

_____

Do you see yourself having the same behaviors and patterns as your
father in relationships? Do you have a similar story?

_____

_____

_____

_____

The Apple Doesn't Fall Too Far from the Tree

Father Essay

Write about any patterns, examples, behaviors, traits, etc., from your father that you duplicated and brought into your last relationship? How did it affect you and your relationship?

_____

_____

_____

_____

_____

_____

_____

_____

_____

_____

_____

_____

_____

_____

_____

_____

_____

_____

_____

Continue free writing on these subjects in YOUR BOOK.

If you find yourself still angry at your father, or any aspect of your relationship (past or present), write an angry letter following the same format as in Chapter 2.

Dear Dad,

_____

_____

_____

_____

_____

_____

_____

_____

_____

_____

_____

_____

_____

_____

_____

_____

_____

Continue free writing on these subjects in YOUR BOOK.

Apple Sauce versus Apple Cider Vinegar

Recognizing Your Parent Wounds

All parents, no matter how conscious they are, pass their material on to their kids. You can choose to blame your parents for all of their mistakes and for where you are at today in life and relationships. You can even pay a professional thousands and thousands of dollars to continue to talk about your story over and over again without moving on.

However, you can also choose to resolve your old childhood issues that affect who and how you are as an adult. In fact, the break-up of your love relationship gives you a perfect opportunity to look deep within yourself to locate your childhood wounds. Ask yourself if your ex mirrors any parts of your father or mother. Ask yourself if your behavior in relationships, the way you react in general, and how your feel about yourself, mirrors your father or mother. In order for you to heal your childhood wounds, take an honest look and an inventory of how your parents have wounded you—if they have.

This is a good time to do an *I Love Them—I Love Them Not Inventory,* like the one we did in chapter 2, or the Resentment Inventory from chapter 4.

I Love Them—I Love Them Not Inventory

Things I HATE about my parent	Who in my life has seen this same trait in me even if they have not said it?	In what way do I own this same trait in myself? (You do.)	How can I not use this trait in my life?

Things I LOVE about my parent	Who in my life has seen this same trait in me even if they have not said it?	In what way do I own this same trait in myself? (You do.)	How can I use this trait in my life?

Resentment Inventory

Write down all the resentments you have for your parents. Continue to do this resentment inventory until you have written down all of your resentments.

I resent	For	It affected my	My part was

Now that you have recognized the hurt that you experienced from your mother and father and your childhood, see how you can find ways to let go and move on. Think about what you learned from your dad and mom. How did your experience with them help you become who you are today? If you've been holding on to feelings of anger or hurt, can you now find a way to love your mom and dad?

Shoulda, Coulda, Woulda Essay

Write a list of all of the things you believe your parents did wrong. Then write how these things affected you then and how they affect you today.

_____

_____

_____

_____

_____

_____

_____

_____

_____

Now, write how you can see the positive in this experience and how you can use it to better your life today.

_____

_____

_____

_____

Are you repeating any of these patterns in your life? [ ] yes [ ] no

Write a gratitude list of all of the things that your parents gave you.

I am grateful for _____

I am grateful for _____

I am grateful for _____

I am grateful for _____

If writing a Gratitude List is a challenge for you, then try this: look for the things they DID NOT give you and ask yourself:
> *• What things would I have not done in life if my parent had given me these things?*
> *• What have I accomplished in life because I had the parents I did?*

_____

_____

_____

_____

GIVE YOUR INNER CHILD HER VOICE
HORTON, HERE'S A WHO ARE YOU

Much of what we're doing in this chapter is getting in touch with the child that still lives in you. What patterns is your little child repeating? How does it act out? Does it pitch fits, yell, scream, have immature knee-jerk reactions, become baby-like to get its way, whine, shut people out to protect him or herself? Is she demanding and manipulative? Acknowledging and listening to that little child within you may be scary, but it is good to know that it needs to be loved. Your inner child needs to be recognized, heard and taken care of. There is nobody better than the grown up you to do this. Don't ignore it. Listen. Try not to let it act out. Tell it that you love it and that you will take care of it. Let it know that it can trust you.

Inner Child Questionnaire

How does your inner child act out?

Identify a piece of wisdom that you would like to give to your inner child.

Taking care of your inner child will allow you to start behaving like an adult. I am not saying that you will never act out again—you are human. But you can start letting the adult in you take charge. Become the parent you always wanted to the little child inside of you. Give yourself the things you always wanted from your parents.

Write your inner child a letter. You might acknowledge how you have neglected it all of these years and how you are going to change. You might want to let it know in what ways you are going to begin to take care of it. Write from the perspective of the parent you want to be. Write whatever you want. Write it from your heart.

Your Letter to Your Inner Child

Dear _____ ,

_____

_____

_____

_____

_____

_____

_____

_____

_____

_____

_____

_____

_____

_____

_____

_____

_____

In and Out Circle
Welcome to the Inner Circle.
If you're in, you're in. If you're out, you're out.

1. On the outside of the circle write all of the things about you and your past relationship that you would like to move on from, not repeat again, and change in yourself and life. (Example: your patterns, behaviors and choices.)
2. On the inside of the circle write all of the things that you learned from the relationship and what you would like to continue to carry into your life and bring into your next relationship.
3. It can be really good to go back to this circle later and see if you are still repeating old behaviors and/or continuing to deepen your strengths.

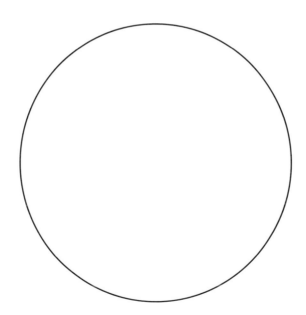

Steven K.

I have to say that I've been in quite a few relationships. Some have ended badly—some not so badly. But, they all ended. Still I have hope that some day the relationship won't have to end. My parents were divorced. Even my grandparents were divorced, which in their day was not the norm, to say the least. But, I still have hope. I think I've learned something from each of my relationships that has gotten me a little closer to realizing that hope. I don't know if the next relationship will be the one. Or the next. But as long as I continue to learn, I still have hope.

Hope—I can see the light!

hope [hohp]

-*verb*

1. to believe, desire, or trust
2. to look forward to with desire and reasonable confidence.

-*noun*

3. something that is hoped for

IN CLOSING

The inner child is you as much as you are the inner child. We might grow older in age and wisdom but sometimes our inner child does not grow along with us. The inner child's growth is stunted because we have a tendency to suppress it. We lock it away in a small dark place, not allowing it the opportunities of a healthy environment. Since we have not healed our inner child within, we allow it to act out in fear and childish ways, which allows us to hurt as adults. We all have the tendency to act like children. Whether your mother or father hurt you, demeaned you, didn't show you love in a way you would have wanted—it's time to reflect, take responsibility for your own life, and find gratitude in knowing that your life has happened the way it has. Now go out and make the best of it.

THE BREAK EVEN

MR. GRAY inspired me to get my
act together financially. I started
to save $. I stopped smoking
when I met him + he helped me
+ encouraged my process w/that.
We took unforgetable trips - up
the coast + Cozumel. first trip I
ever paid for w/o my parents.

I WENT TO GRADUATE
SCHOOL !!! This was decided
when we were
in a relationship.

AND OUR BREAK UP triggered
me to do more work on MYSELF

I WE WHAT I learned to con
grow + walk into my
self.

My book is BETTER &
RELATIONSHIP w/ him

6

-Phrasal Verb
1. to finish a business transaction, period of gambling, series of games, etc., with no loss or gain.
After losing all night at the craps table, the gambler finally broke even and cashed out.

The Break Even stage happens when you have gained the necessary knowledge to accept your past.

> ### *You've gotta know when to hold onto them, when to let go of them, when to walk away, when everything is okay...*

The Break Even stage is about letting go—even when it seems that things are already over. Many of us tend to hold onto a lot of negativity over relationships, long after we have convinced ourselves that we have let go of them. Letting go is a process. It's not just as easy as saying it out loud. Sometimes it takes work—including looking at both the relationship's positives and negatives as well as your own. Through honesty with both, you can transform the negatives into future positives. In doing so, this "work" can be inspiring, because you are becoming more self-aware and are able to find the gifts in yourself and the ones your relationship presented to you. After all of this, you might even find the gratitude for your break-up.

LAW OF ATTRACTION...
POSITIVE + NEGATIVE + YOU = POSITIVE

"We are what we think,
all that we are arises with our thoughts.
With our thoughts we make the world."
—Buddha

As human beings our minds are constantly in motion—both logically and creatively. Your Left Brain is random, intuitive, holistic, synthesizing, subjective, and looks at wholes. Your Right Brain is logical, sequential, rational, analytical, objective and looks at parts. Whether logical or creative, our thoughts make our world. Our world is made up of internal stimuli (thought) and external situations. It is important to learn that you can choose how you process these thoughts—either negatively or positively. Your negative thinking will become a negative reality and your positive thinking will become a positive reality. Your life becomes exactly what you think of and put attention on. This is The Law of Attraction: Negative thoughts generate negative emotion and draw negative life experience. Positive thoughts generate positive emotion and draw positive life experience.

"Loving people live in a loving world.
Hostile people live in a hostile world.
Same world."
—Wayne Dyer

We attract everything that comes into our lives. We manifest these things because we hold the image in our mind. Whatever is going on in your mind, you attract. Example: If you want a new job, you go out and buy the Sunday paper, take out the career section and start circling jobs that you can easily acquire. Then you build a resume, make calls and appointments, get dressed appropriately, show up on time, and do the best job you can in the interview. It all starts with a thought in your mind. Then you have to take the actions to get there. If you really want something in life and put your attention on it, that is exactly what you will get.

The same rules apply when you continue to dwell on negatives. For example, you say, "my life is full of drama and chaos." If you continue to think this way, without doing any thing to change it, then your life will be dramatic and chaotic.

Let's say you tell your friends and family that you are ready to heal your broken heart, and that you're sick and tired of dealing with the drama your last relationship brought you. Meanwhile you are still talking to your ex on the phone every day, you still have a deep desire to be with him, and you are not taking any actions to heal and move on. You are still involved in that relationship, repeating the same patterns and behaviors from before, and you will continue to hurt. If you want to heal your broken heart, then focus on the healing and whatever you have to do to heal.

> *"What things soever ye desire,*
> *when ye pray, believe that ye receive them,*
> *and ye shall have them."*
> —Mark 11:24

This same magnetizing thought process applies to your love relationships. If you believe that nobody loves you, all men cheat, all women are whores and gold diggers, love never lasts, and everyone gets divorced, then this is what you will create as your reality.

The point is, we always have a choice. Even in difficult times we have a choice of how we handle our thoughts. The trick is seeing the good in the bad. If you are having difficulty in grasping how to shift your thinking to attract love, abundance, positivity, and good in your life, then begin trying or pretending. Say, "I don't get it right now. But maybe today will be the day that I do." Or, if you feel down, depressed, lost, scared and confused, you can ask for guidance by saying, "I know that my relationship is over but maybe today will be the day that I can see a brighter future and put a smile on my face."

If you want to be healed, then begin to heal yourself. Do the work on yourself. I don't mean that you should struggle. If you feel the drive to do this work, it won't feel like work at all. You will be inspired. You will love to do it because you will see results.

Start believing that your heart is already healed. Envision what that is like for you. Focus on your future and what it is going to look like. Decide what kind of person you want to become. What does this look like?

Say the following affirmations and feel free to create your own as well:

- I am full, beautiful and whole.
- I am doing great.
- I am on a journey towards wholeness and my Best Self.
- I am taking actions to heal my broken heart.
- I have forgiven the pains in my past and have received the gifts in them.
- I love who I am becoming.
- I have a new love for myself.
- My heart is healed.
- God helps those who help themselves.

This can all be a reality if you love yourself. This is your reality if you believe it.

SELF: 101
BECOMING YOUR OWN SELF
OR:
CATERPILLAR TO BUTTERFLY

"Today you are You, that is truer than true.
There is no one alive who is Youer than You."
—Dr. Seuss

Who Do You See Your Individual Self to Be?

in_di_vid_u_al_ [in-*duh*-**vij**-oo-uhl]
-noun
1. a single human being, as distinguished from a group.
2. a person: a strange individual.
3. a distinct, indivisible entity; a single thing, being, instance, or item.

Synonyms:
atypical, avant-garde, bizarre, conspicuous, cool*, curious, eccentric, eminent, exceptional, extraordinary, loner, noteworthy, odd, oddball, onliest, original, out-of-the-way, outlandish, outstanding, peculiar, prodigious, puzzling, queer, rare, remarkable, special, strange, three-dollar bill, uncommon, unimaginable, unordinary, unparalleled, unprecedented, unthinkable, unusual, unwanted, weird

As you've been seeing throughout this book, during a break-up you get to take charge of your emotional self and your life. You can begin to learn and recognize the many different aspects of you. You get to explore and blossom into the unique individual that you are. You get to expand, extend, mature, discover, realize, develop, and become autonomous. In finding your own voice, you have the opportunity to explore, study your soul, and experiment with different things that you may enjoy. This can all lead to transformation.

It's time to start listening for those important questions about your core being that tend to arise during times like this—your life's purpose and what and who you want to be in this world. Perhaps you've already started having more vivid dreams since you started working with the material in this book. Perhaps you've been taking notes in YOUR BOOK. The following questionnaire can help you better understand you.

Who Am I Questionnaire

Who am I?

_____

_____

_____

_____

Do I see the glass as half empty or half full?

_____

_____

_____

_____

How am I different?

_____

_____

_____

_____

What do I believe?

_____

_____

_____

_____

How do I experience life?

_____

_____

_____

_____

How do my actions and behaviors affect others and who do they make me in this world?

_____

_____

_____

_____

How am I a part of my environment?

_____

_____

_____

_____

How do my views differ from my family and friends?

_____

_____

_____

_____

How can I become more myself?

_____

_____

_____

_____

Continue free writing on these subjects in YOUR BOOK.

Most of us have gotten so good at fulfilling a role or various roles—in order to satisfy the demands of family, lovers, friends, and society—that we can forget that these are often masks. They are not who we are at our core. Your mask mediates between you as a person and the world around you. We create masks in order to think, feel, and behave in the ways we think others want us to, or that we think we should. You might wear a mask in the beginning of a love relationship so that the other person will love you more. You may become who you feel they want you to be.

The mask you created to survive in this world might have done a good job of protecting you from the environment you grew up in. But now there may be many layers of yourself undiscovered or hidden behind your mask. At some point you will realize how painful it has been to hide away so much of yourself. To truly become your authentic self, it can be helpful to take your influences as lessons and incorporate them to find your own voice and unique potentials. You can choose to leave your conditioning behind. This does not mean that you have to erase all of it from your memory and mind. Speaking your own mind does not mean that you have to alienate yourself from your family and friends. What it does mean is that you can find your own voice and create your own beliefs and conditioning. In fact, you can learn to acknowledge, accept, and appreciate other people's individuality and ask that they do the same for you.

Your conditioning and all that you have experienced has brought you to where you are today. **What you resist in life persists.** If you ignore your past like it does not exist, then it will continue to creep up on you in different ways (i.e. in the different people that you meet, and in your unconscious behaviors).

The Mask Questionnaire

Who is the stranger that has been living behind your mask? What personality does it have?

_____

_____

_____

_____

What and who would you be if you could be who and what you want to be?

_____

_____

_____

_____

Continue free writing on these subjects in YOUR BOOK.

There is not one single person in this universe like you, and the only person who knows what is good and important for you, on many different levels, is you. Of course discovering your individual self doesn't happen overnight—it is a lifelong journey. This does not have to be an overwhelming or bad thing. In fact, it can be exciting to continue to seek, discover, and become a person with your own voice. If you begin to understand the different aspects of you, you will be able to create much deeper and fulfilling relationships. In allowing your true self to emerge, you can become open to different experiences, someone who trusts their intuition, someone who is constantly growing and blossoming, while becoming the person that they want to be in this world.

My Personal Individual Personality Profile
Or:
Enough about Me—What about Me?

I am: (Below are some examples. Circle the ones that apply to you.)

outgoing	shy	popular	nerdy
smart	stylish	city person	career person
homebody	funny	simple	loud
quiet	traveler	athletic	artsy
bookworm	tv watcher	eccentric	scientist
musician	pet lover	sexy	neat
sloppy	sophisticated	educated	uneducated
self-aware	unaware	boring	strong
guardian	nurturer	caregiver	doer
performer	artist	executive	scientist
visionary	thinker	giver	protector
inspirer	idealist	classy	introvert
talker	spiritual	religious	messy
clean	interesting	dramatic	cool

Continue free writing on these subjects in YOUR BOOK.

Fill in the blank:

I feel _____

I want _____

I need _____

I wish _____

I am _____

I dislike _____

I like _____

I love _____

I hate _____

I aspire to _____

I dread _____

I support_____

I believe _____

I doubt _____

I accept _____

I regret _____

I am proud of _____

I am ashamed if _____

I am against _____

I am addicted to _____

I am special because _____

I am _____

Are you most comfortable: (check whatever applies to you)
[ ] Alone   [ ] In large groups   [ ] In crowds

[ ] Socializing   [ ] In small groups   [ ] At work

[ ] With Family   [ ] Helping others   [ ] Observing others

In social situations you are: (check whatever applies to you)
[ ] quiet   [ ] life of the party

[ ] approaching people [ ] waiting for people to approach you

Write down four words that describe you?

_____

_____

_____

_____

What are your four best qualities?

_____

_____

_____

_____

What are your four worst qualities?

_____

_____

_____

_____

What are four things in your life that you regret?

_____

_____

_____

_____

What are four things in your life that you are proud of?

_____

_____

_____

_____

What do you hate?

_____

_____

_____

_____

What do you love?

_____

_____

_____

_____

What are some patterns and behaviors in yourself that you would like to change?

_____

_____

_____

_____

What are the actions you can take to change them?

_____

_____

_____

_____

Define who you are in a relationship:

_____

_____

_____

_____

Define who you would like to be in a love relationship:

_____

_____

_____

_____

How can you achieve being this person?

_____

_____

_____

_____

Continue free writing on these subjects in YOUR BOOK.

Self-Awareness Essay

Who are you? Who do you believe yourself to be? What makes you unique in this world?

_____

_____

_____

_____

_____

_____

_____

_____

_____

_____

_____

_____

_____

The Break Even

_____

_____

_____

_____

_____

_____

_____

_____

_____

_____

_____

_____

_____

_____

_____

_____

_____

_____

_____

_____

Continue free writing on these subjects in YOUR BOOK.

Carole L.

When my relationship ended, I couldn't accept it—I wouldn't accept it. How dare he break up with me. I had never been broken up with before. I was always the one doing the breaking up. I knew there were problems in the relationship. That was obvious, but nothing I couldn't handle. But, as time went on I began to accept the fact that it was over. Our problems were probably something I couldn't or shouldn't have handled. We just weren't meant to be.

> **Acceptance**—*I'm ready for* whatever comes
> ac·cept·ance [ak-sep-*tuhns*]
> *-noun*
> 1. the act of taking or receiving something offered.
> 2. favorable reception; approval; favor.
> 3. the act of assenting or believing: *acceptance of a theory.*

GIFTS
BOW. RIBBON. WRAPPING PAPER. BOX. PACKING PAPER. THE RELATIONSHIP. IT'S THE THOUGHT THAT COUNTS.

"Life is the first gift, love is the second, and understanding the third."
—Marge Percy

Mirror, mirror on the wall, what's my greatest gift of all? As difficult as it may be to hear right now, your ex and your break-up is the greatest gift you have been given—in this moment. Even in the most excruciatingly painful lessons in life lie gifts; it's just a matter of us becoming aware of them. No matter how you feel about your relationship right now, I suggest that you begin to see it as one of the greatest gifts that you have ever received. This gift is that your ex, your experience in the relationship, and even the fact that it ended can help you become a more evolved person. Being with your ex awoke these gifts in you. You have gained more knowledge, tried new things, and gotten to know yourself better. Now it is your chance to take that knowledge and do something with it.

It is easy to find gratitude in life when things are going well—like when you first fall in love (La La Land). It might seem more challenging to be grateful when life isn't going in the direction that we think it should—like when a break-up happens. You think, "Why do I deserve this?" Or, "It's unfair." However, this is the time when the greatest gifts can be received. If you look deep enough, there will be something there. You can experience an awakening. When one door closes, another always opens. If you are not grateful for what you have been given, then how can you expect to be given more?

Mirror Mirror Questionnaire

Your ex is a mirror reflection of you in many ways, and mirrors speak nothing but truth. What did your ex mirror in you?

_____

_____

_____

_____

Know and remember this: each and every person you allow to enter your life is a mirror reflection of something in you. This is a gift for you to understand and get to know more parts of yourself.

_____

_____

_____

_____

Gifts Essay

What gifts have you received from your relationship?

_____

_____

_____

_____

_____

_____

_____

_____

_____

_____

_____

_____

_____

_____

_____

_____

_____

_____

_____

_____

_____

_____

_____

_____

How can you utilize these gifts to better your life?

_____

_____

_____

_____

Face it. It isn't just in love relationships that we have mirror reflections in our lives. We have them in friendships, with family, siblings, co-workers, etc. Who are some people in your life that are a mirror reflection of you?

_____

_____

_____

_____

What qualities about you have they made you aware of (both negative and positive)?

_____

_____

_____

_____

What gifts can you get from your experience with them?

_____

_____

_____

_____

Now that you are aware of these gifts, how can you use them to better your life?

_____

_____

_____

Throughout this book you have been reflecting on things in your life that at the time seemed difficult, negative, and challenging. Now, look at these experiences with your newfound knowledge, and find the gifts in them. List these experiences and the gifts they gave you. Next to the gifts, write how you can utilize them in your life.

_____

_____

_____

_____

_____

_____

_____

_____

_____

_____

_____

_____

Continue free writing on these subjects in YOUR BOOK.

Once you truly begin to feel this relationship as a gift, you won't feel the negativity of the break-up weighing heavily in your life. You are more likely to see the gifts when you are balanced and centered within yourself. Try to focus on the things from the relationship that you are grateful for. I'm not talking about sugar coating or glossing over the negatives, rather holding them in balance with the positives. When you can see the negative and positive in a situation, you are no longer a victim, always tense, on red alert and shut down. You are free.

> *"Every person who has ever come to you*
> *has come to receive a gift from you.*
> *In so doing, he gives a gift to you—the gift of your*
> *experiencing and fulfilling Who You Are."*
> —Neale Donald Walsch

Kate E.

A couple of break-ups ago, a friend suggested that I do a gratitude list. She thought it would help. I thought she was crazy, so I protested. But, good friend that she is, she persisted. So I figured, what the hell, it couldn't hurt. Come to find out, she was right. It did help—TWO BREAK-UPS LATER! Better late than never to find the gratitude.

> Gratitude—I'm so thankful
> **grat·i·tude** [**grat**-i-tood, -tyood]
> *-noun*
> the quality or feeling of being grateful or thankful
> I suggest that you continue to write your gratitude lists.

Writing a Thank-You-for-the-Break-up Letter

Earlier in the book, we talked about writing an angry letter to your ex, as part of your process of honoring all your feelings. Now it's time to write your ex a gratitude letter, telling him how grateful you are that you got to experience life with him in the time that you did. Tell him the gifts he brought you. Tell him the things you would never have seen or accomplished if it weren't for him. You do not have to send this letter. In fact, I don't necessarily recommend it. However, if you do decide to mail this letter, recognize what your expectations are. Do you have an agenda in sending the letter (ex. To win him back, or to prove to them how much you've grown, etc.)? Or, do you have something to say because you cherish the relationship and you don't need to get a response back from him? This letter is intended for you and your growth.

My Thank You for the Break-up Letter

Dear _____ ,

_____

_____

_____

_____

_____

_____

_____

_____

_____

_____

_____

_____

_____

_____

_____

_____

_____

_____

_____

_____

_____

Continue free writing on these subjects in YOUR BOOK.

Remember, "Mirror, mirror on the wall, what's the greatest gift of all?"

The last relationship that you were in is a gift. Open it. Receive it.

"Let us rise up and be thankful, for if we didn't learn a lot today,
at least we learned a little, and if we didn't learn a little,
at least we didn't get sick,
and if we got sick, at least we didn't die; so, let us all be thankful."
—Buddha

One for me. Two for you.
What goes around, comes around.
Karma. Karma, Karma.

"It's better to give than receive."
—Jesus Christ

Now that you have received these gifts, why not give some charitable gifts? It can't hurt. Give of your time and energy to some positive ventures. You can start as close as home or as for away as an international relief fund. You don't necessarily need to join the Peace Corps, but giving to others never hurts. It might just be babysitting for a friend, helping out with a project, giving your time at your local church or school, or just spending time with someone in need. There is no shortage of people who need help, and it just might make you feel good.

IN CLOSING

The thing about The Law of Attraction is that it's easier said than done. We would all like to attract only positive in our lives. But, the truth is that we attract negative things into our lives because of habit. It takes work to stop attracting negativity and start attracting the positives that are out there for all of us. In saying this, we can learn and grow from the negatives that come into our lives—if we so choose. When we look at the transformation of the catepillar to butterfly, we look at the caterpillar as the negative and the butterfly as the positive—when they are actually one in the same. The only real transformation was through their growth in the chrysalis stage (the Break Even stage). Through your increased self-awareness, you may now find your past relationship(s) as gifts through which you may learn to be grateful for your break-up.

THE BREAK THROUGH

Some of my VALUES:

- Honest & accountable
- commitment – I commit.
- Creative
- Personal internal growth
- following my dreams & my heart.
- faithful.
- competative
- family / friendships
- fun / travel
- spirituality
- earnig & career
- good listiner
- Service to others
- having a comfortable

7

-Phrasal Verb
1. To make a sudden, quick advance, as through an obstruction.
2. pass through (a barrier)
3. penetrate; "The sun broke through the clouds"
4. To achieve a breakout.
After hours of digging, he broke through the wall to freedom.

The Break Through happens when you find gratitude and become your Best Self.

Break on through to the other side.
Or: Don't worry, be happy.

The Break Through stage is your opportunity to take all that you've experienced through the previous stages and make them work for you. You're no longer in a break-up, you're ready to break through. That does not mean that you are through with your growth. In fact, it means that you are just beginning.

FUTURE
NEVER PUT OFF UNTIL TOMORROW WHAT YOU CAN DO TODAY BECAUSE TOMORROW ALWAYS COMES.

Confucius says, "Be the master of your own destiny because if you don't do it who will?"
—Anonymous

fu_ture_ [**fyoo**-cher]
-noun
1. something that will exist or happen in time to come: The future is rooted in the past.
-adjective
2. that is to be or come hereafter: future events; on some future day.
3. pertaining to or connected with time to come: one's future prospects; future plans.

As many opinions as there are on what the future holds, and as complex as the future is, the only belief that is true is the belief that is true *for you.* Whoever you perceive yourself to be is who you are. However you believe your future will unfold is probably how it will unfold. It is all a matter of perception. Our thoughts create our reality.

Easy for me to say! In fact, I've already said it. But it bears repeating. If you believe that everyone is out to get you, that all men cheat, that you have no luck, that all women are sluts, and that there is no hope for you, then that is exactly what you will get. If you believe that you can accomplish certain goals and dreams, that you can work through challenging times, and you see that there is light at the end of your tunnel, then that is what will happen.

PERCEPTION
IF GOD GIVES YOU LEMONS, MAKE LEMONADE, PROCESS IT, PACKAGE IT, LABEL IT, MARKET IT, SELL IT, AND ENJOY THE PROFITS.

This isn't just my fantasy. People who believe they can have a good life do have a good life. They believe that they can accomplish things that they really want and walk through life with their heads held high. It's not that such people manage to get through life without challenges. It's that they manage to handle those challenges.

Have you ever been in a car with a person who gets angry in traffic or yells at the person in the car next to him—for not driving faster or driving too fast or cutting him off or whatever? Consider this: There is probably another driver in the same traffic jam who passed the same person your companion yelled at but is totally unaffected. Because he knows there is absolutely NOTHING he can do about the traffic. He knows that he will get there when he gets there. Perhaps he gives himself ample time to get where he is going. Once again, it is all about perception. Our perception creates our reality. If you believe your glass is half empty of lemonade, then so it will be. And if you believe it is half full, then it is.

Positive vs. Negative Questionnaire
Write down a time in your life when you were in a negative situation and kept living in the negative.

_____

_____

_____

_____

What could you have done to turn that negative situation into a positive one by changing your attitude?

_____

_____

_____

_____

List some positive people and how they handle negative situations and turn them into positives.

_____

_____

_____

_____

Continue free writing on these subjects in YOUR BOOK.

The moment you change your perception is the moment your life can change. This all goes hand in hand with the work you have been doing in this book. If you have been paying attention, your perception has probably changed about your life, yourself, and the people around you. The same goes for your future. No matter what you perceive your future to be, that is probably what you will get. You might ask, "Why don't I always get what I want?"

You might not always get what you ask for, but you do always get what you create. With this perception, you get to take charge of your life.

Whatever you truly, truly work hard for, and believe that you will have, is what you will create.

When a person makes a living doing what she loves, she does not give up, she does not give in, and she insists on doing it. That's what we're talking about here. Not magical thinking but a belief that we can and will grow internally, we will do everything in our power, and everything that feels right to us, to do so. The person who has no clarity, no goals, is unsure of himself, and has a lack of follow through, will probably have more difficulty creating what he wants. It is all a matter of choice.

It is important to be clear with yourself about what kind of a future you want to create for you. So how do you get such clarity?

Visualize

"The biggest adventure you can ever take
is to live the life of your dreams."
—Oprah Winfrey

Begin by asking yourself what you want your future to look like. Then start being who you want to be.

Here's one approach that can help: Go find a comfortable place to lie down or sit comfortably. When you get there relax, breathe, and close your eyes. Imagine the person you want to be—your future self. **VISUALIZE.** When you see a clear picture, ask yourself the following questions and write down your answers.

Who is your future self?

_____

_____

_____

How do you feel?

_____

_____

_____

What are you doing?

_____

_____

_____

Continue free writing on these subjects in YOUR BOOK.

You can become this person. Do whatever it takes, whatever you can, to become that person. From this moment forward, question yourself about everything, and continue to ask yourself what parts of you still need to grow. Take your whole self into consideration: your values, goals, work, balance, fulfillment, family, and life purpose.

Do you want to stop limiting yourself to achieve your future goals?
[ ] yes [ ] no

If your answer is yes, the following questionnaire can help move you along towards your future self.

Future Self Questionnaire

What are the most dominating issues in your life that stand in your way of being that self?

_____

_____

_____

_____

Are there people standing in your way of having or achieving what you want out of life? [ ] yes [ ] no

If yes, who and how do they stand in your way?

_____

_____

_____

_____

What is missing in your life that would make it more fulfilling?

_____

_____

_____

_____

If you did not have anything holding you back, what would you do?

_____

_____

_____

_____

Who or what inspires you?

_____

_____

_____

_____

What famous person or people do you admire? Why?

_____

_____

_____

_____

What activities do you enjoy doing most?

_____

_____

_____

_____

What are your greatest achievements in life?

_____

_____

_____

_____

What have you really wanted, gone after, and then gotten in life?

_____

_____

_____

_____

What did you do to get it?

_____

_____

_____

_____

What is your proudest moment in life?

_____

_____

_____

_____

When you were a child, who or what did you want to be when you grew up?

_____

_____

_____

_____

If money were not an issue and you could choose any career, or careers, what would it or they be?

_____

_____

_____

_____

What kind of special knowledge or experience do you have?

_____

_____

_____

_____

What are your greatest priorities in life and why?

_____

_____

_____

_____

How meaningful is your life today? Do you feel a purpose, excited, bored, challenged, living, not living, able to achieve your goals or not, etc.? Explain:

_____

_____

_____

_____

*How meaningful do you want your life to be? What is your person-
al vision for your future?*

_____

_____

_____

_____

Do you feel pessimistic or optimistic about your future?
[ ] pessimistic [ ] optimistic

*Are you interested in doing any volunteer or charity work? If so,
what kind?*

_____

_____

_____

_____

Continue free writing on these subjects in YOUR BOOK.

INTENTION
SEE IT TO BE IT

intention_ [in-**ten**-sh*uhn*]
-*noun*
1. an act or instance of determining mentally upon some action or result.
2. the end or object intended, purpose.

To become the person you want to be you have to set an intention for yourself, visualize becoming that person, and take whatever steps along the way to get there.

Many people drift day to day, week to week, month to month, and year to year, with confusion, little focus, or any long-term direction. Others sometimes have a goal, sometimes achieve it, sometimes not, and other times don't have any clarity, hope, direction, or ambition to get there. And then there are those who live their lives with specific goals and a vision, with rigid daily planners, post-its all over their house and office as reminders, to do lists, and time management self-help books and seminars. These are people who have an intention. (You can have an intention without overdoing it. Balance. Balance. Balance.)

www.mapquest.com—Map Questing Your Life

You can have all the dreams you want, but in order for you to make your dreams come true, in order to manifest them in your life, it is important to make your dreams into a clear visual picture. I suggest that your life's vision be complete and focused. It is also important to ensure that your vision is what YOU really want—not what your family, boyfriend, girlfriend, ex, friends, a teacher, or society want for you. This does not mean that you can't change your mind along the way. You might have a dream or a goal, take the steps that you create for yourself, and then discover that you want to do something else along the way, or that you no longer want to do it. That's your right. However, if you do change your mind, make sure that you question yourself about why. Are you running away from something? Do you have a tendency to run away from things, do you have a fear of achieving things that you want? Do you feel unworthy of having it?

Maybe you had a teacher who told you that you will never make anything out of yourself and that you can't read and write. Maybe you had a parent who told you that money is bad. You might have been told that work is awful and you have to work your butt off just to get food on the table. Maybe this is your reality at the moment. But it does not have to continue to be your reality. Whatever negative thoughts were instilled in you as a child for you to obtain your dreams, it's time to get past them. Whatever limiting ideas you came to believe don't matter anymore because all they are doing is blocking your road to the amazing life that could be yours. Sometimes we have to take a detour (your path to overcome the negativity of a particular situation) to get to our ultimate destination.

Setting intentions for yourself and learning how to achieve them is one important way of changing your life. One way of doing this is by setting goals. Some goals are day-to-day, while others will be long term. Plant a rose garden, take a road-trip across America, cook and prepare a new dish for dinner, have a family of your own, get a new job, get into shape and lose 10 pounds—or 100—learn a new language, write in your journal every day, become more organized, or finish this book. Setting goals can help you find direction and live the life you want. By knowing what you want, you get to choose where you want to focus your energies. By having direction, you can also be more aware of the things that would otherwise lure you from your direction.

So many people are ready for change in their lives but they are unwilling to make changes within themselves. Therefore, they and their situations stay the same.

Mapquesting Your Life Questionnaire

Who in your past told you something that blocks you from obtaining your dreams? What did they say or do?

_____

_____

_____

_____

_____

Did you ever overcome this? [ ] yes [ ] no

If no, can you find a way to get past what they told you? [ ] yes [ ] no

If yes, name some actions you can take to achieve those dreams now.

_____

_____

_____

_____

_____

Is there anything stopping you from achieving your short-term or long-term goals now? What is it?

_____

_____

_____

_____

_____

What has stopped you from achieving your goals in your past?

_____

_____

_____

_____

_____

How do you limit yourself?

_____

_____

_____

_____

_____

What has that cost you?

_____

_____

_____

_____

In what ways have you benefited from limiting yourself?

_____

_____

_____

_____

_____

Are you willing to stop limiting yourself? [ ] yes [ ] no

What are the actions that you can take to stop limiting yourself?

_____

_____

_____

_____

Are you still carrying any baggage that is weighing too heavily on you to allow you to move forward? [ ] yes [ ] no

If yes, what can you do to unpack that baggage to move forward?

_____

_____

_____

_____

_____

When you are ready...you choose the time for you...move forward. You are here now, so you might as well make the most of it.

Oh, the places that you've been.
Oh, the places that you were.
Oh, the place that you are.
Oh, the places that you can go.

What were your biggest disappointments last year?

_____

_____

_____

_____

_____

What did you learn from those disappointments? Name each one and what you learned.

_____

_____

_____

_____

_____

What were your greatest accomplishments last year?

_____

_____

_____

_____

_____

What did you learn from those accomplishments? Name each one and what you learned.

_____

_____

_____

_____

_____

What did you do to achieve those accomplishments? Name each one and next to it describe the actions that you took.

_____

_____

_____

_____

_____

What did you learn?

_____

_____

_____

_____

_____

_____

What actions do you take that work?

_____

_____

_____

_____

_____

_____

Do you need more discipline anywhere?

_____

_____

_____

_____

_____

_____

Are there any areas in your life where you are not achieving what you want? (financial, love, family, staying in shape, job, living situation, etc.)

_____

_____

_____

_____

_____

_____

Do you limit yourself? [ ] yes [ ] no

If yes, how can you stop limiting yourself?

Continue free writing on these subjects in YOUR BOOK.

Your Intentions

"I will do my best to be
honest and fair,
friendly and helpful,
considerate and caring,
courageous and strong, and
responsible for what I say and do,
And to
respect myself and others
respect authority,
use resources wisely
make the world a better place."
—Scout Law

Your Value Areas

Your values are integral in determining who you are and helping you get where you want to go. Without values you would be lost. Your values areas are what motivate you. They motivate you to get out of bed in the morning. They motivated you to buy this book. Examples: self-preservation, self-awareness, etc. You may not be conscious of all of your underlying motivations; but the more that you are conscious of them, the easier it is to change your life. List your values in order of importance: Personal Growth/Spiritual, Fun/Recreation, Health/Physical, Career, Financial, Relationship/Love, Family/Friends, and Environment.

On a scale of 1–10, how do you rate yourself in each area right now? Write your number in each area. Write down how much time per week you spend in each area. Write the number you want to have in each area. Then write how much time you want to spend each week in that area.

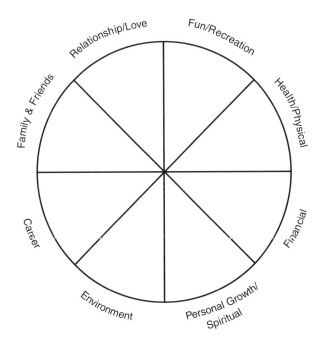

What are the steps you need to take to get to the number you want to achieve in the following areas in your life?

Personal Growth/Spiritual:

_____

_____

_____

Fun/Recreation:

_____

_____

_____

Health/Physical:

_____

_____

_____

Career:

_____

_____

_____

Financial:

_____

_____

_____

Relationship/Love:

_____

_____

_____

Family/Friends:

_____

_____

_____

Environment:

_____

_____

_____

Writing down or typing your intentions on a piece of paper finalizes them, gives you a sense of accountability, and can help bring order and direction into your life. Expand your vision by visualizing.

Set intentions in all areas of your life:
> *Your Individual Self*
> *Family*
> *Home*
> *Friends and Social Life*
> *Financial and Career*
> *Spiritual*
> *Physical and Health*
> *Mental*
> *Educational*

I dream my painting and then I paint my dream.
—Vincent Van Gogh

What roles do you play in life? Naming your roles can help you see what is important to you.

Daughter	Friend	Cook
Student	Worker	Dancer
Runner	Lover	Artist
Counselor	Yogi	Decorator
Financer	Spiritual Advisor	Teacher
Mediator	Adventurer	Etc.
Etc.	Etc.	Etc.

What are your responsibilities?

_____

_____

_____

_____

_____

What kind of map do you want to create for you to get on your journey towards your intention and your vision?

1. Set an intention.

2. Make your intention official by writing it down.

3. "I am" statements can help in this process. (Example: I am in a loving and conscious relationship.)

4. Create a map of how you can achieve that intention. These are the small steps and goals that you can take to achieve this intention. (Example: One step would be to begin dating, tell friends that you are available to date, joining a dating Web site, etc.)

5. Name the obstacles that can get in your way (what could go wrong, where, when, and with whom) and what you can do to prevent it from happening or move through the obstacles.

6. Follow through with the steps on your map. Don't get discouraged. If you don't follow through one day, get back on it as soon as you can.

1. My intention:

_____

_____

_____

Steps I need to take to get there.

_____

_____

_____

_____

These are the obstacles that can get in my way and what I can do to prevent them or move through them.

_____

_____

_____

_____

_____

_____

_____

2. *My intention:*

_____

_____

_____

Steps I need to take to get there.

_____

_____

_____

_____

These are the obstacles that can get in my way and what I can do to prevent them or move through them.

_____

_____

_____

_____

_____

_____

_____

3. *My intention:*

_____

_____

_____

Steps I need to take to get there.

_____

_____

_____

_____

These are the obstacles that can get in my way and what I can do to prevent them or move through them.

_____

_____

_____

_____

_____

_____

_____

4. My intention:

_____

_____

_____

Steps I need to take to get there.

_____

_____

_____

_____

These are the obstacles that can get in my way and what I can do to prevent them or move through them.

_____

_____

_____

_____

_____

_____

_____

5. *My intention:*

_____

_____

_____

Steps I need to take to get there.

_____

_____

_____

_____

These are the obstacles that can get in my way and what you can do to prevent them or move through them.

_____

_____

_____

_____

_____

_____

_____

6. My intention:

_____

_____

_____

Steps I need to take to get there.

_____

_____

_____

_____

These are the obstacles that can get in my way and what I can do to prevent them or move through them.

_____

_____

_____

_____

_____

_____

_____

7. *My intention:*

_____

_____

_____

Steps I need to take to get there.

_____

_____

_____

_____

These are the obstacles that can get in my way and what I can do to prevent them or move through them.

_____

_____

_____

_____

_____

_____

8. *My intention:*

_____

_____

_____

Steps I need to take to get there.

_____

_____

_____

_____

These are the obstacles that can get in my way and what I can do to prevent them or move through them.

_____

_____

_____

_____

_____

_____

_____

Continue free writing on these subjects in YOUR BOOK.

Once you are finished writing down your intentions and the steps to get there, tape them to your wall, put them on your fridge, put them in your day planner. You can also copy them and place them in a goal or treasure chest or put them in your Box. Whatever you do, follow through with your action steps. I have mine written on a card that I keep by my bedside. I see it first thing when I get up in the morning and last when I go to bed at night.

VISION BOARD
GOTTA SEE IT TO BE IT

*"Star Light Star bright,
the first star I see tonight,
I wish I may, I wish I might,
have the wish I wish tonight."*
—Nursery rhyme, author unknown

A Vision Board is a great way for you to visualize and for your sub-conscious to reveal to you what you want out of life. The action of doing this activity helps manifest these things into happening.

To create a Vision Board, you will need magazines, glue, tape, poster board, and any other collage material you would like to use. Grab a bunch of magazines (old or new), flip through the pages, and cut out the images, items, and words that speak to you. Include pictures that look like the person you want to become (hairstyle, outfit, body size, hair color, glow, job, house, family, etc), places you want to travel, the life you want to live, the kind of house you want to live in, the things you want to own, and anything else you want to add. Collage all of these things that you want to have in your future on a poster board. Hang your completed collage in a place where you can see it. You now have a vision of the things you want to manifest. Wait patiently—things do not happen overnight.

*"Life is just a bowl of cherries, don't take it serious, it's mysterious.
Life is just a bowl of cherries, so live and laugh and laugh at love,
love and laugh, laugh and love."*
—Bob Fosse

Tommy F.

Freedom is something that you earn. It took me a while to realize this. My last boyfriend broke up with me because he said that I didn't give him enough freedom. I didn't get it. Freedom from what? I loved him. I wanted to spend all my time with him. HELLO!!! WE WERE IN A RELATIONSHIP!!! I mean why be in a relationship if you don't want to be together 24-7?

Okay, so I was a little codependent. In retrospect, a little bit of freedom is a good thing. I think at the time I just wasn't happy with me. And, when I was alone the only person I had to judge was me. These days I'm happier with my life because I'm happier with being me. Now I enjoy some freedom of my own because I've done the inner work to earn it.

"Free at last! Free at last! Thank God almighty, I'm free at last!"
—Martin Luther King, Jr.

The NOW WHAT? Essay

Now that you are single, what do you want to do with your life? Speed Write whatever comes to your mind, without censoring.

NOW...

_____

_____

_____

_____

_____

_____

_____

Continue free writing on these subjects in YOUR BOOK.

"You had the power within you all along."
—Glenda the good witch from *The Wizard of OZ*

IN CLOSING

Your perception is extremely important because how you see life affects how you live life. But just as important are the actions you take—how you work through situations in your life. Without setting an intention, following through with your action steps, and knowing what your values are, you cannot achieve the life you would like to live. Most importantly, never put off 'til tomorrow what you can do today. Because tomorrow comes every 24 hours and you might as well be ready for it when it does. It's your life—so live it.

"Just when you think tomorrow will never come, it's yesterday."
—Anonymous

The End
Book One: *Break-Up Emergency*™

The Journey Continues…

The Beginning
Book Two: *Dating Emergency*™

DATING

EMERGENCY

A guide to transform ME into WE by dating consciously

"It's the heart afraid of breaking that never learns to dance.
It is the dream afraid of waking that never takes the chance.
It is the one who won't be taken who cannot seem to give.
And the sould afraid of dying that never learns to live.
—Bette Midler

THE STEPS

—noun

1. A move, act, or proceeding, as toward some end or in the
general course of some action; stage, measure, or period: the
12 steps to dating consciously.

2. To move, go, etc. To make or arrange in the manner of a
series of steps. *I took the necessary steps to get where I was
going.*

3. An offset part of anything. *There were many steps to
achieve the goal so I took them one at a time.*

The Guide to Transform ME to WE by Dating Consciously

Break step
- Why we long for an intimate relationship.
- Looking at the history of relationships from then to now.
- The different archetypes of relationships.
- How times have changed in "the rules" of dating.

Keep Step
- The who, what, when, where, why of relationships—i.e., what makes a conscious relationship?
- The myth of soul mate.
- The fairy tale of La La Land.
- The Yin and Yang Thang.
- Putting your relationship in context.

Step Forward
- To move forward, you must start by taking the first step.
- Getting ready for love.
- Setting an intention to begin dating again.
- Putting it out there in the Universe that you are open, willing, and ready.
- The values wheel—what is important to you.
- Defining what you want in a mate.

Step Aside
- The Law of Attraction. Kicking your pessimism to the curb and giving your optimism a hug.
- Reconnecting with who you are and how you affect your relationships.
- Taking responsibility for yourself and your life!!!
- Defining what you have to offer.

Step Back

- Discovering your old baggage and learning to deal with it.
- Growing from your experiences. What type of mate do you continue to attract into your life and why?
- Settling your old external conflicts. He said—She said.
- Putting the past in its place—in the past where it belongs.
- Redefining what you want in a mate.

Step Out

- Stepping out of being alone.
- Being the person you want to find.
- Preparing yourself to step into being with others.

Step In

- Stepping into being with others.
- Continuing to have your own hobbies. Don't lose the ground that you've gained.
- Having oneness and separateness with your partner.

Out of Step

- Feeling out of step back in the dating game.
- Changing your dating habits—going where you've never gone before.
- Losing yourself in another is losing you.
- Falling in love with Mr. X again.

In Step

- Finding your rhythm in dating again.
- La La Land all over again. First impressions can be first illusions.
- Finding yourself "in step" with someone—what to do.

Step down
- Reevaluating your values and your mate's.
- Should I stay or should I go?
- Stepping down from a relationship that is not working for you.
- Not letting saying "Good-bye" be the hardest thing to do.

Step up
- Moving the relationship forward.
- Intimacy—the many levels and questions.
- Commitment—the many levels and questions.
- Reality Land—its ins and outs and ups and downs.

Step by step
- Growing. Love never stays the same.
- Working through being out of step.
- Facing challenges by communicating. CommuniDATE—set a date to communicate.
- Taking the steps you need to take to keep your relationship conscious.
- Reevaluating your reevaluations.
- Remembering: It takes two to tango.

The Next Step...

EMERGENCY
CONTACT INFORMATION

Suicide Prevention

National Suicide Prevention Hotline

1-800-821-4357

www.cdc.gov/safeusa.htm

Alcohol and Drug Dependence

National Alcohol and Drug Helpline

1-800-821-4357

National Council on Alcoholism and Drug Dependence

1-800-423-4673

www.ncaad.org

Alcoholics Anonymous

1-800-923-8722

Domestic Violence

National Domestic Violence Hotline

1-800-799-SAFE

National Resource Center on Domestic Violence

1-800-537-2238

Domestic Violence Notepad

www.womenlawyers.com/domestic.htm

Emergency Contact Information

Sexual Abuse
RAINN—Rape, Abuse, and Incest National Network
1-800-656-HOPE
www.rainn.org

Eating Disorders
American Association of Anorexia and Bulimia
1-212-575-6200
www.aabainc.org

Pregnancy/AIDS/STDs
Planned Parenthood
1-800-230-PLAN
www.plannedparenthood.com

National CDC STD and AIDS Hotline
1-800-227-8922

General Mental Health/Therapy Referrals
National Mental Health Consumer Self-Help Clearinghouse
1-800-553-4539

National Mental Health Association Resource Center
1-800-969-6642

Women's Health
National Women's Health Network
1-202-629-7814
www.womenshealthnetwork.org